Creed and
Personal Identity

Creed and
Personal Identity

*The Meaning of the
Apostles' Creed*

David Baily Harned

FORTRESS PRESS   Philadelphia

Biblical quotations, unless otherwise noted, are from the Revised Standard Version of the Bible, copyrighted 1946, 1952, © 1971, 1973 by the Division of Christian Education of the National Council of the Churches of Christ in the U.S.A., and are used by permission..

The Apostles' Creed on page 12 is reprinted from the *Service Book and Hymnal* of the Lutheran Church in America © 1958.

Library of Congress Cataloging in Publication Data

Harned, David Baily.
  Creed and personal identity.

  1. Apostles' Creed.   I. Title.
  BT993.2.H37   238'.11   80–8056
  ISBN 0–8006–0645–0

8274F80   Printed in the United States of America   1–645

Contents

5

Introduction

Identity Avowal

These pages explore the meaning of that part of the Christian faith which is set forth in the Apostles' Creed. I understand the gospel to be the story of who Jesus Christ is and of what he does, together with the assurance that everything he is and does, he is and does for us. The perspective from which this book is written is Protestant and finds in the theology of John Calvin and Martin Luther a most important expression of the richness of the Christian tradition. The several occasions for this theological exposition have afforded neither reason nor opportunity to examine the historical development of the Creed, to explore its antecedents, or to survey all the varied functions it may originally have performed. These are important questions, of course, but it is nonetheless possible to explicate the theology of the Creed without giving attention to them.

This essay is contributed to the commemoration in 1981 of the sixteen-hundredth anniversary of the second ecumenical council of the Christian church, which was held at Constantinople in 381. In Constantinople, the fathers reaffirmed the unity and triunity of God which the first ecumenical council had asserted at Nicaea in 325, clarified this fundamental teaching in a way that prepared for the great affirmation at Chalcedon in 451 of the perfect union of divinity and humanity in Jesus Christ, and proclaimed that in the earthen vessels of the Nicene deliberations, and therefore also in the Apostles' Creed, the treasures of the faith were expressed for every generation until Christ comes again. Constantinople inaugurated fifty years of relative tranquillity during the formative centuries of the church, tranquillity predicated upon agreement that in

7

Jesus Christ God had come among us and disclosed the unchanging splendor of his triune nature in the work of our redemption.

The contention which distinguishes these pages from many other essays on the Creed is that the Creed's substance cannot be satisfactorily interpreted apart from attention to the twin questions of its function and its form. The answer offered to the first is that the Creed is primarily neither a summary of Christian beliefs nor a sort of loyalty oath, but instead is a statement of our identity as people who have been born anew through the Spirit and now live in Christ. Belief statements, loyalty oaths, and identity avowals are not mutually exclusive, but we shall discover persuasive reasons to insist that the Creed is vulnerable to serious misunderstanding if it is not recognized as first of all the latter. In no way, however, is this claim in conflict with the enduring conviction of the Christian community that the Creed is speaking of what is wholly other than ourselves.

We would scarcely honor the intentions or actions of the fathers at Constantinople if we were to permit the question of the formation of a sense of identity to imply the dissolution of everything into the problem of self-understanding. In fact, our sense of identity depends upon nothing else so much as upon the otherness of that to which we are related, and upon the fidelity with which we are enabled to grasp that otherness in its distinction from ourselves. There is no help or hope for us, unless they are ultimately different from the help and hope we can give ourselves. The Creed is one of the great treasures of Christian faith because, in the end, its subject is not the individual, not the community, not anything at all—except God.

The answer to the second question is that the Creed shares with the New Testament a form which is essentially narrative. Christianity is not first of all a world view but a story; insofar as contemporary rationalism inside and outside the church has misunderstood this, it has mistaken shadow for substance and mislaid the riches of the gospel.

The Creed gains its narrative quality from its reflection of the biblical recital of the works of him who is not only an individual but, in his historical particularity, also a new Adam who repairs all that the old Adam has done. But this emphasis upon narrative and therefore upon the life of the imagination is not intended to qualify or obscure the truth claims that generations of the faithful have asserted for the Creed. If its witness to the everlasting truth of human affairs were to require revision today more than it did a century or even a millennium ago, it would be far less important, as well as far less exciting, than it remains—and there would be little reason, if any at all, to commemorate what the church affirmed at Constantinople in 381.

The answers offered to the two questions concerning the function and form of the Creed play important roles in shaping the nature of the exposition and they are undergirded by a claim more fundamental still: the importance of particulars, which are the stuff of which narrative is made and with which a sense of identity is concerned. William Blake once wrote, "No truth, save only Particulars." This is far from the whole truth, of course, but there is much truth in it—and especially truth that the Christian tradition must assert, for it knows no substitute for the flesh, blood, and bone of a particular man. An argument that informs all these lectures is that the business of theology is with the particular rather than the general, the definite instead of the abstract, narrative structure and not propositional form, images in preference to concepts.

Images and concepts are both cognitive devices, but the concreteness and vividness of the former render them far more consequential for human affairs. Images and stories are correlative: the latter interpret images in ways that relieve them of their ambiguities, while the former crystallize the significance of narratives for the exercise of the self's choice and agency. Images and stories contain a great untidiness of nuance and connotation, and so they are endowed with a greater cognitive density than the concepts and propositions from which all this messiness has been chipped away. But this untidiness can organize the messiness of our actual existence in ways that propositions and injunctions cannot. Therefore, our concern is with the story of God's acts for our redemption, the great images that can fortify our sense of identity as Christian people, and the particular and concrete individual in whom God's decision for us and our salvation is made known and fulfilled.

In the course of this exposition, then, a small army of presuppositions can be discerned, busily bullying recalcitrant odds and ends or sweeping bits and pieces into dark corners. But, even though we can acknowledge the power of our assumptions, none of us can elude it entirely. These chapters are intended simply to explore the theology of the Creed with the most useful devices at hand, not to examine and attempt to justify the devices in abstraction from the Creed itself. It is best, perhaps, to try to allow its substance to question the validity of the questions we ask. Those who are particularly interested in these presuppositions will find them discussed in an earlier work, *Images for Self-Recognition*. It should also be mentioned that the epilogue which constitutes chapter 9 is intended only for those who wish to pursue further the question of master imagery for the formation of a Christian sense of identity, and therefore it may be safely omitted by those whose interests are confined to the actual text of the Creed. Its contents have been expressed much more systematically and expansively in *Images for Self-Recognition*.

The lectures on the first article were originally delivered in a different form in various contexts in India. Among numerous and generous hosts there, I am particularly indebted to three very good friends—M. S. Nagaraja Rao, director of archaeology and museums in the state of Karnataka, and Harbans Singh and Lal Mani Joshi, both of Punjabi University, Patiala. A revised version of the same talks constituted the Westervelt Lectures for 1979 at Austin Presbyterian Seminary. I am most grateful for the invitation extended to me by its president and vice-president,

Jack Maxwell and Jerry Tompkins, for the graciousness of its faculty and students, and especially for the matchless hospitality of my friends Hallie and George Heyer. Subsequently, the lectures also furnished a topic for discussion at the 1979 meeting of Duodecim, where Julian N. Hartt presided with his usual wit and grace. More recently, a number of colleagues in Scotland have read and commented on the entire text; I am very much indebted to Thomas F. Torrance, D. W. D. Shaw, Iain R. Torrance, Alasdair I. C. Heron, and especially to Ian Breward, a colleague from Dunedin, New Zealand. The inadequacies that remain in the essay, however, I can claim as all my own.

The Apostles' Creed

I believe in God the Father Almighty, Maker of heaven and earth:[1]

And in Jesus Christ his only Son our Lord, Who was conceived by the Holy Ghost, Born of the Virgin Mary, Suffered under Pontius Pilate, Was crucified, dead, and buried: He descended into hell;[2] The third day he rose again from the dead; He ascended into heaven, And sitteth on the right hand of God the Father Almighty; From thence he shall come to judge the quick and the dead.[3]

And I believe in the Holy Spirit;[4] The Holy catholic Church, the Communion of Saints; The Forgiveness of sins; The Resurrection of the body, And the Life everlasting.

NOTES

1. Early Greek versions, unlike the developed Latin form of the Creed, speak of the "Maker of all" in a way that emphasizes the continuing creativity and providential activity of God more strongly than the Latin does. Both forms are addressed in the text that follows.

2. These words were a very late addition to the Creed and their original meaning is obscure. They are, nonetheless, of very considerable theological significance.

3. In the so-called Nicene Creed, these words are followed by the clause, "Whose kingdom shall have no end." Brief attention to this is given in the following text, as a theological preface to the concluding words of the Apostles' Creed.

4. The text refers to "Spirit" rather than "Ghost," in accordance with prevailing usage. More importantly, an "And" serves to preface the third article. This was included in the earliest Greek forms of the Old Roman Symbol, from which our Apostles' Creed developed, and its theological significance later becomes explicit in the clauses of the so-called Nicene Creed, "Who procedeth from the Father and the Son, Who with the Father and the Son together is worshipped and glorified."

1

"I Believe in . . . "

Master Image

Apart from Scriptures and sacraments, no element within the Christian tradition has been so greatly revered and widely employed as the Apostles' Creed. Interpretations of it have been many and various, however, and between Roman Catholic versions and those that have emerged from the Reformed traditions there has been a fundamental distinction. The former typically assume that the three articles of the Creed are arranged in the order in which their subjects are known. But the Reformed traditions teach that there is a difference between the *ordo essendi* and the *ordo cognoscendi:* the subject of the first article, while primary in the order of being, is actually last in the order of knowing. In other words, Christians do not first arrive at faith in a Creator, while only thereafter affirming faith in the Son and Spirit; instead, it is through the agency of Son and Spirit that they are enabled to worship and glorify the Creator. This Protestant perspective, which will find frequent expression in these pages, means that no article can be regarded as though it were more or less independent.

In this chapter, we shall examine the meaning of the words "I believe," which introduce us to the ingredients of a sense of personal identity. Conventional wisdom assumes that the Creed is a summary of beliefs to which Christians assent when they recite its words. Because other religious traditions have not developed summaries like ours, the Creed distinguishes Christian community not only materially but formally. Christianity is different not only because of its particular beliefs but also because of its propositional statements of belief to which adherence is mandatory. I want to argue against this conventional assumption, however, and explore other ways in which the Creed can be understood. Beliefs are a secondary and derivative aspect of community, not the principal source of its strength. The Creed is more fundamental to the welfare of the church, and a proper interpretation of it can suggest analogues in every other religious tradition.

We must briefly address three topics, the first of which is the "relational" nature of our humanity. To the eyes of a skeptic, the Creed seems quickly to slide from the light of certainty and certitude into the obscurity of ever greater uncertainties. There is the certainty of the existence of the self and there is the self's own certitude of its beliefs, but all else is uncertain and beyond verification. How is it possible that these things could seem credible, in the light of all the randomness, accidents, and pain that desolate our life together? Christians must also ask how it is possible, but in a way that directs the question toward the believer rather than the beliefs. Why is it *given* to me to believe? Surely the capacity to believe must be understood as a gift, for I am not unacquainted with the terrible griefs and ruined designs that are the human lot. As the aged black priest reflects in Alan Paton's novel of South Africa, *Cry, The Beloved Country* ([New York: Charles Scribner's Sons, 1948], p. 274): "Why was it given to one man to have his pain transmuted into gladness? Why was it given to one man to have such an awareness of God? And might not another, having no such awareness, live with pain that never ended? . . . He put it from his mind, for it was a secret."

To phrase the same question in a different way, why is it given to *me* to believe, for I am entirely unworthy of such a gift? Whoever pronounces the first word of the Creed does so only because that person has seen his or her own portrait in the confession of Paul that "I am carnal, sold under sin. I do not understand my own actions. For I do not do what I want, but I do the very thing I hate. . . . I do not do the good I want, but the evil I do not want is what I do" (Rom. 7:14–15,19). To ask the same question in still another fashion, then, who *is* this self that believes? We are enabled to do something that we could never do by ourselves, and not only in the sense in which a child might be emboldened to undertake some new challenge because of the supportive presence of a parent. Instead, each of us must confess, "I, yet not I, but Christ in me." There is no way to understand our own conduct and nature except through Jesus Christ.

So the apparent certainty with which the Creed begins— the existence and identity of this person who affirms that he or she believes—in fact enshrines mysteries orchestrated with ever greater intensity. There are the assurances of our election and God's grace, a bestowal of gifts as unexpected as they are undeserved. There is the ambiguity of the person, whose identity is obscured because of the warfare within the sinful self and enriched because of the christological reference required by acts that exceed the self's own powers. The mysteries of divine election and grace and of human identity and agency are all summoned into the forecourt of vision by the utterance of the first word of the Creed. This "I" itself denotes a miracle, for in the believing "I" are encountered powers gracious and more than human, who could never be reached had they not first condescended to touch the landscape within the fractured self that hitherto had been only, in the words of Matthew Arnold's "Dover Beach," "a darkling plain/Swept with confused alarms of struggle and flight."

As the preface to the Creed, the word "I" suggests much more than human agency and initiative, for the self exercises its choice as it does only because it has first been chosen. The point is not only that initiative resides always with God, although this is surely true, but that we become what we are because of the ways that we are or are not enabled to respond to God's initiative. So our identity is not an item established or a position long secured. Because we have been far from God, the terrain within the sinner has strange beasts and treacherous portages and places where the sun never shines. Because we have now been brought near by powers beyond our own, we can no longer be described apart from Jesus Christ. Indeed, identity has an eschatological dimension, for "it doth not yet appear what we shall be" (1 John 3:2 KJV) when Jesus comes again. The apparent certainty with which we began already appears thoroughly uncertain, because the first person singular is a reflection of that to which it is related, and its potential relationships are limitless and as radically different as the daimonic and the divine.

Secular wisdom can recognize the relational character of our humanity, but Christian reflection upon the preface to the Creed furnishes its own quite independent and entirely theological reasons for the conviction. The human venture is a relational affair: identity is not achieved by the self primarily through the exercise of its own resources but is a gift from others, developed through a complex of relationships and, decisively, through the self's relationship to Jesus Christ. It is through our activity, however, that our nature is expressed and confirmed or changed, and so we must address a second topic that raises the whole question of how the Creed can best be understood. What does it mean to "believe," for in this exercise the self's agency is first disclosed?

There are at least three ways to interpret the Apostles' Creed. Perhaps they are not exhaustive and certainly they are not mutually exclusive, but one will inevitably dominate the others. The first is the conventional understanding of it as a more or less systematic statement of beliefs. This approach has been severely criticized, however, especially by Wilfred Cantwell Smith, who argues that it attaches to "believing" an unfortunately modern significance. In *Belief and History*, he contends that the "I believe" is really analogous to the "I do" of the marriage rite. *Credo* is derived from *cor*, heart, and *do, dare*, to give; its meaning was to swear loyalty or pledge allegiance. Modern English usage, however, has obscured this element of commitment, as attention has shifted from the orientation of the subject to the status of the object. So it no longer functions as once it did, when it denoted "a promise, and bore no resemblance to the descriptive propositionalism of a modern theorist's reporting on the current state of his opinions." Ironically, a verb that was first intended to denote the certainty of commitment is now employed to convey objective *un*certainties, "dubious, or at best problematic, propositions."

This and similar criticisms of the conventional interpretation of the Creed gain persuasive support from the curious omissions that have long been remarked in the text. The most important of these, perhaps, is the lack of any reference to the condition from which we are redeemed. This absence is crucial, for the law is the insistent counterpoint of the gospel and the richness of the latter is not intelligible apart from it. Typically, in the so-called parallel between the first Adam and Jesus as a new Adam, Paul writes that "Law came in, to increase the trespass; but where sin increased, grace abounded all the more" (Rom. 5:20). Again, there is no mention of the history of God's transactions with Israel, the covenant with Abraham, or the Davidic ancestry of the Messiah. But how can the New Covenant be understood without reference to the Old? The church has long agreed that it cannot.

Because of omissions such as these, the Creed is sometimes regarded as a response to a heresy that unsettled the church at Rome in the second century. It appears to emphasize the catholic view of issues debated in the second-century struggle with Marcion. Because it was shaped by controversy and therefore did not incorporate points that were not contested, it is less than a systematic summary of the faith. Few scholars remain persuaded by this thesis, for the early connection of the Creed with baptism was so intimate that it must be understood as designed primarily for the enrichment of the community and not simply for the repudiation of inadequate interpretations of the faith. Nevertheless, the magnitude of its omissions, which once seemed excellent evidence that it was a polemic against heresy, still furnishes a powerful argument against the claim that it is, in fact, a compendium of basic Christian beliefs.

If the Creed is not a belief statement, what is it? Professor Smith views it as a pledge or loyalty oath. Belief statements and loyalty oaths intersect, in the sense that when we claim to believe in a friend, we affirm not only our loyalty but also our conviction that certain beliefs about the friend are true. Where the emphasis lies is important, however, for in belief statements there is an implicit acknowledgment of uncertainty concerning the object of belief. In contrast, whatever uncertainties appear in connection with loyalty oaths can have as their focus nothing except the orientation and performance of the subject. But significant difficulties confront the attempt to treat the Creed as a pledge, for this interpretation stumbles upon omissions as perplexing as those which confound the first approach. There is no portrayal of the Christian way of life and no mention of the cruciality of prayer, of gratitude as the motive for conduct, or of love of neighbor. For those instructed only by the Creed, Christianity might well be construed as privilege without responsibility. Much the same might seem true of certain secular oaths like the pledge of allegiance to the American flag; in this instance, however, there are tacit obligations that are conventionally understood, such as liability to taxation and military conscription. But when the Creed was formulated, there was no consensus among catholics and followers of Marcion about the shape of the Christian life. So the absence of any reference to the meaning of discipleship is all the more anomalous because there was no undisputed understanding of it at the time.

Another difficulty that confronts this approach is the integral connection of the Creed with baptism. If the sacrament were a rite of passage that marked the transition from youth to maturity, the importance of a loyalty oath as an avowal of responsibility would be indisputable. But baptism has a different significance: it is not a time for the display of maturity but a moment when someone is "born again" as a child. It is an occasion when God promises to be faithful even when the children of God are faithless, and constant despite all their inconstancy. So the Creed must not be understood in some legalistic way, as though it were the last human contribution that the divine operation presupposed. There can be no doubt that the Creed functioned in relation to sacraments and theological instruction as a learning device and also as a pledge of loyalty. But perhaps it served in these ways because it performed another function more fundamental still.

Although it has affinities with both belief statements and loyalty oaths, the Creed is first of all *an identity avowal*. In other words, "I believe" is primarily an acknowledgment that the self stands in a relationship to God, sees itself always in the light of God's inescapable presence, subordinates to this all other elements of its understanding of itself, and therefore derives from this situation its own sense of identity. The confession refers both to the reality of the object, as in belief statements, and to the orientation of the subject, as in loyalty oaths. But the whole is much more than the sum of its parts. It refers also to the orientation of the object, God's own faithfulness, and to the new nature and sense of identity the self derives from its incorporation into Jesus Christ. This "I believe" denotes the most decisive relationship the self knows and, because its sense of identity is formed through and reflects its relationships, the words become a confession of who the self is.

At baptism, the person who is born again and launched upon a different childhood is given a new name. The new name is "child of God." All children must gain a sense of and taste for the identities their names describe and grow familiar with the relationships and histories in which their names involve them. Even though years may pass before a child can intelligently utter its words, the Creed is a crucial factor in the formation of a Christian sense of selfhood because it is an avowal of a new identity in relation to the larger identity description of Jesus Christ offered by the Bible and presented anew in the preaching, sacraments, liturgy, and prayers of the community. The Creed serves as a window to Scripture and directs attention to the identity description there; its recital follows from and more deeply acquaints those who employ it with the biblical picture of Jesus as a concrete universal—both *a* man and *man*, a new Adam in and through whom our own humanity is found. In this context, "I believe" means that people find the story which lends coherence and significance to their lives in the biblical narrative of Jesus, their history and future in his history and future, and therefore their sense of identity in relation to the whole story of the Bible.

This interpretation of the Creed can account for the otherwise perplexing absence of any reference either to the condition from which sinners are redeemed or to the nature of redeemed existence. The omissions that remain stubbornly unintelligible when it is approached in some other way become inconsequential when it is viewed as an identity avowal dependent upon a larger identity description, because now there is no reason for it to be more than a sketch or reminiscence of the richness of the biblical narrative of Jesus. It cites the beginning and ending of the story and stresses the central dramatic action of the cross and the resurrection. Nothing more than the essential structure of the narrative is necessary; it is the biblical drama itself that is intended to clothe these bones with flesh and endow them with life. The Creed is intended simply to serve as a transparency to that inexhaustibly richer text.

Perhaps the nature of the Creed as an identity avowal can be clarified in the light of a comment upon the writings of Paul by a contemporary biblical scholar, Hans Conzelmann. He tells us that

> Paul has a positive understanding of theology as exposition of the faith. The faith is formed in doctrinal sentences, to be sure, but these sentences interpret the existence of the be-

liever. The credo is only interpreted if it is seen that the objective statement about Christ contains a statement about myself (including my future). This is indeed its meaning for the Corinthians.*

Whether or not Conzelmann is entirely correct in his analysis of this logic of self-involvement in the New Testament, his reflections are illuminating because of their similarities and dissimilarities to this approach to the Creed. The early church did not distinguish consistently between preaching and teaching, or *kerygma* and *didache*, and sometimes the Creed was described as the former rather than the latter. But there is an important difference between the gospel and the Creed that points toward and sketches the biblical story.

Although Conzelmann is correct to insist that the New Testament is not "a quasi-timeless core of the truths of faith and non-historical definitions," it must be remembered that in the *kerygma* the objective statement is primary and commanding, while the element of self-involvement is entirely secondary and subordinated to it. In the Creed, however, the objective statement is presupposed, the "I believe" is primary, and its meaning is that the self interprets itself from *within* the objective statement. Because the self now stands within the story, the narrative is not susceptible of doubt and there is no possibility of disaffiliation from it without the loss of the self's sense of identity. So the element of self-involvement has become a logic of self-definition. This "I believe" is not a preface to a series of "dubious" propositions that Christians must affirm—in which case it would confront us as law instead of grace. Neither is it an expression of the self's own commitments that finally directs attention toward the subjectivity of the individual. On the contrary, precisely *because* it is an identity avowal its words orient us toward the objective statement that it presupposes, direct our gaze toward that with

* Hans Conzelmann, "On the Analysis of the Confessional Formula—1 Cor. 15:3–5," *Interpretation* 20, no. 1 (January 1966): 24.

which we are now identified, and tell of the indisputable power of this narrative to transform personal existence.

In conclusion, we must turn briefly to a third topic that is integrally related to our earlier comments on the relational nature of the self, and discuss the process through which we develop a sense of our own identity. It arises from the imagination's portrayal of the self's solidarity with and distinction from what lies beyond itself. We begin to see ourselves in relation to parents, then to peers and teachers, shopkeepers and visitors, and finally to a variety of institutions, interests, values, and still other figures of authority, some of whom are represented in the internal dialogues of the self with itself even though they have never been encountered except at secondhand. From these relationships we harvest the images of ourselves that afford us a sense of identity, shape our will, and render our freedom concrete.

Imagination describes neither a single power or faculty of the self nor merely the source of its dreams and fantasies, but the sum of all the resources that we employ to form accurate images of ourselves and our world. *Image* denotes a representation of reality, either internal or external to the self, that has a concreteness and vividness not easily matched by concepts and a cognitive density that propositions do not attain. So it is wrong to regard imagination as though it were an untrustworthy guide to serious affairs. Because its works display the whole range of our powers, because they have a richness that concepts cannot equal, and because they are more consequential for the exercise of our freedom than even the most urgent injunctions, imagination is not the artificer of illusion but rather our means of access to truth. In the end, truth is something we must *do*, and imagination rules the ways we use our freedom.

We belong to nature as well as history, of course, and from our bodily commerce with our environment we also gain images that contribute to our sense of identity. But the most important ones are socially derived; among them, images of the self have a certain priority over images of the world, for all our perspectives are established in and through our imagery of the self and its functions and roles. How we see the world, and thus are enabled to act within it and react to it, depends upon the sense of identity we have gained from our various relationships, for self-images furnish the point of vantage from which we shall appraise everything else. There are problems that beset the development of a sense of selfhood, however, and two deserve particular mention in treating the Creed as an identity avowal.

First, the images of ourselves that we gain from our different relationships frequently conflict with one another. They achieve a measure of integration only insofar as they are dominated by one or more *master* images that can qualify and reconcile other imagery, so that identity becomes less protean than it would otherwise be. These master images bring to self-consciousness the implicit narrative quality that life sometimes discloses and therefore motivate the self to seek ever greater measures of coherence and consistency—in other words, to develop character. The second problem is that images can be enigmatic and elusive, like a light so dazzling the eye that the beholder is temporarily blind. This ambiguity is ordinarily resolved because important images are associated with stories that interpret them and, indeed, it is the stories that persuade us of their importance. Stories can resolve the ambiguity of images without cost to their concreteness, while images can capture the significance of the stories for the exercise of our freedom.

Our relationships afford us many and competing stories that are replete with images of selfhood—stories of race, nation, and family, of economic and social failure or success, of bodily prowess or frailty. We have also, in the Bible, the story of the works of God. For those who are aware that they stand in a relationship to the triune God, the Apostles' Creed provides a master image that relativizes and promises to integrate all other self-images. As God is Father, so is the person a *child of God.* Yet this image is so ambiguous and elusive that it is liable to great distortion if it is not rigorously defined in relation to the narrative of the covenant that is fulfilled in Jesus Christ and concludes with the promise of his return to judge living and dead. As a sketch of the biblical narrative, the Creed reflects its form. "I believe" indicates that the self accepts as its own story the narrative that clarifies this master image so that it can offer integration where there has been none and bring liberty to the captives.

In theological perspective, then, "I believe" does not refer primarily to the status of the object; the reality of the story and its capacity to transform the individual are beyond dispute, although only the eyes of faith can see that its power is not only the power of all good stories but also the power of Father, Son, and Holy Spirit. Nor does "I believe" refer first of all to the orientation of the subject. In one of the works of Ignazio Silone, a mother bids farewell to a son who is going off to war. She tells him that if he brings honor to her she will be very proud, but that if he does not she will still be his mother. This is the heart of the biblical story: God's constancy despite the inconstancy of those who claim "I believe" but whose faith fades and flickers like the light of a fire. If "I believe" is also an expression of commitment, it is much more an acknowledgment of the faithfulness of Jesus toward those in whom the old Adam struggles still, but who nonetheless can see themselves as each a child of God. The Apostles' Creed has been incomparably important in the Christian tradition precisely because it did not originally serve as a propositional summary of the faith. It has begun to seem less significant only as it has been misunderstood by modern rationalism inside as well as outside the church.

2

"God the Father"

Root Metaphor

The first chapter was devoted to the twin claims that the Creed is primarily an identity avowal rather than a belief statement or loyalty oath, and that for the development of a Christian sense of selfhood it provides the master image of *child of God.* In the context of a portrayal of identity formation as the appropriation of images of ourselves that we derive from our relationships, "I believe" was regarded as an acknowledgment that we stand within and understand ourselves from a relationship to God. This interpretation can account for the omissions that seem unintelligible if the Creed is construed in other ways, because as an identity avowal it is inseparable from the biblical identity description of Jesus Christ. Christian obedience and creaturely disobedience are described together in the narrative about him of which the Creed is simply a reminder and a sketch.

This approach offers a distinctive perspective for the interpretation of the relationship between Christian community and other religious traditions. What seemed a formal distinction between them, the absence of binding summaries of belief in propositional form from the latter and their importance in the former, is not of decisive significance if, in fact, the Creed is first of all a resource for community formation that must necessarily have analogues in other traditions. The differences between religious communities do not reflect *primarily* a divergence of beliefs, although beliefs certainly differ, but the various ways in which selves have been socialized to perceive their own identities. The heart of the matter is the problem of identity formation and the stories, images, and root metaphors that are partly expressed and partly obscured when they are enshrined in belief systems or fragments of belief systems. The primitive church knew that beliefs are a subordinate aspect of community, for it was acquainted with the biblical warning that even the devils believe. The truly formidable dimension of community is not its power to shape the beliefs of its members, but its capacity to determine their vision of the self that believes.

The first of three topics that we must now explore is the meaning of the preposition which follows the introductory verb. Long ago, Peter Abelard distinguished between three sorts of belief: *credere Deum, credere Deo, credere in Deum.* The first denotes belief *that* God exists, the second indicates belief *in* God as purposive and consistent in his acts, and the third means the heart of the believer is wholly dedicated and oriented toward God. Only the latter, Abelard insists, is "saving faith," the work of grace. The difference between "believing that" and "believing in" is important, for the former frequently can leave the center of selfhood untouched and the latter can sometimes transform our lives. But the distinction is always tentative and provisional, for beliefs are certainly among the factors that determine our conduct and the loyalty expressed by "believing in" necessarily involves a cognitive element. We believe *in* a friend because we are sufficiently acquainted with the person to believe *that* our trust and loyalty are not misplaced. "Believing in" entails truth claims; if it did not, Christian faith would be blind, indeed.

Nothing is more precious, more commonplace, more potentially hazardous than our countless experiences of "believing in"—in friends and family, in neighbors and nation, in these values or those causes, in science or history, or in the prowess of the self. Faith is a pervasive ingredient in human affairs; if there were nothing to believe in, there would be no reason to do anything at all. Some instances of "believing in" are more important than others, however, and sweep lesser commitments to the periphery of vision. Believing can be a dangerous venture; Luther properly warns us that whatever our hearts trust and confide in

can become an idol. Even though it is evident that many
powers in which we believe are rendered neither daimonic
nor divine by our activity, believing always contains the
potential to create false gods. This is part of the significance of Abelard's second distinction, his insistence that
"believing in" is not necessarily sufficient or, to phrase it
differently, that there are different sorts of "believing in."
Sometimes "believing in" is less than what God requires
and sometimes it forges the tyranny of an idol. But the
possession of a false god is invariably punished, for the
self's idolatry is reflected in its constricted sense of its
own identity, and in actions that inevitably separate it from
other people and diminish its possibilities.

How is it possible that we should prefer lies to truth,
pursue illusion instead of reality, and make our own gods
rather than worship the God who made us? We do
so because we find ourselves surrounded by worthwhile
causes and challenging goals, by many different sources of
pleasure, by many tasks that promise a measure of fulfillment. We must choose among them, sifting the more important from the less, and sacrificing some for the sake of
others worthier still. The most important occasionally become *centers* of value from which we appraise our own
worth and the worthwhileness of everything else. So family
and nation, for example, become not only values that we
acknowledge but also sources of the perspectives from
which we sometimes assess our own careers and the significance of all our other relationships. In other words, our
commitments contain implicit identity avowals whenever
we surrender ourselves entirely to the perspective of the
cause or community or other value that has exacted our
allegiance. Then we become wholly one with our family or
nation, and see ourselves in no other way.

When some relationship that is valuable and sometimes *a*
center of value is consistently perceived as *the* center of
value, however—when the self regards it as not only the
greatest good but also as the source of all good, including
the goodness of the self itself—the continuum of our relationships is ruptured and we become the victims of an idol.

No matter where this center is found, it establishes a sense of identity that is divisive, destroying community and setting the self against its neighbor. As H. Richard Niebuhr has shown in *Radical Monotheism and Western Culture,* the welfare of the center always requires that we not only love its allies but also hate its enemies and remain at least indifferent toward everyone and everything the center does not include. When the center is mislocated anywhere within the finite realm, the self's sense of identity is constricted and finally lost. One image of the self excludes all that are not wholly in its service, while the imagery that remains is no more than a tedious repetition of the master image. Everything falls away until the self is nothing but its single tyrannical relationship and has no identity but this.

God demands the same exclusive devotion that idols exact, but the consequence is an inclusive commitment that false gods never permit. The Creed teaches that God the Center is Father, the Almighty, the Creator. Because he is Father, the self finds itself within a universal structure of kinship. Because he is the Almighty, nothing can finally threaten the fulfillment of God's familial design. Because he is Creator, all that is, is valuable; everything must be respected and cherished because all of it comes from the hand of God. So the other side of the exclusiveness that God requires is a qualified but inclusive commitment by the self to the whole creaturely universe, whether human or part of the human environment, actual or ideal, present or yet unborn. Only in God can we discover a center of value that does not blind the self to and isolate it from aspects of its world and elements of itself. Unlike imagery conferred by false gods that diminishes and withers a sense of identity, the image of the child of God opens the possibility of a whole galaxy of subordinate images derived from relationships with everything to which the self is kin. Each of them can offer its own enrichment to a Christian sense of identity, for all express our relation to what God wills and sustains.

"I believe in God the Father." Our second topic is the *root metaphor* that justifies the master image. A root metaphor is

the source of a particular angle of vision upon everything else whatsoever—not only the holy but also the human, not only their intersecting histories but also the natural context in which revelation occurs—and the notion is borrowed from *World Hypotheses,* by Stephen C. Pepper. Although history seems to exhibit a bewildering variety of "world hypotheses," Pepper argues that the philosophical imagination is far less prolific than it first appears. In fact, many ostensibly different theories are expressions of the same root metaphor, and there are actually no more than four "distinct ways in which men have seriously undertaken to build up unrestricted hypotheses" concerning their world. A root metaphor, he continues, is developed because

> A man desiring to understand the world looks about for a clue to its comprehension. He pitches upon some area of common-sense fact and tries if he cannot understand other areas in terms of this one. This original area becomes then his basic analogy or root metaphor. He describes as best he can the characteristics of this area, or, if you will, discriminates its structure. A list of its structural characteristics becomes his basic concepts of explanation and description. . . . He undertakes to interpret all facts in terms of these categories.*

The differences between this interpretation of the philosopher's quest and the discipline of Christian theology are as obvious as they are profound, but Pepper's work is of great importance because of its stress upon a single, seminal image or metaphor that structures the self's vision of itself and of everything else. No matter how different or even irreconcilable various Christian theologies may appear, they all finally display a common identity derived from the shared root metaphor of the fatherhood of God. This is not one divine attribute among many, but a principle for the interpretation of them all. It shapes every dimension of the Christian vision, enabling us to see our-

---

* Stephen C. Pepper, *World Hypotheses* (Berkeley: University of California Press, 1942), p. 91.

selves as God's children, the world as a home, other selves as members with us of one family, sacraments and sacramentals as instances of new birth or occasions of familial reconciliation or correlates of familial times of crisis, and one's own family as both relativized and consecrated by the everlasting fatherhood of God.

The familial imagery that the root metaphor provides is in no way intended, however, either to restrict God's operations to human families or his caring to the human race. The whole Bible testifies to the particular and unflagging concern of this Father for all who are widows or orphans or otherwise excluded from the households of man, and Jesus himself is a paradigm of the outsider. The creativeness of God more than justifies the wonderful canticle in which St. Francis jubilantly sings of his kinship with "brother Sun" and of his gratitude for moon and stars, "precious, bright, and fair." Christian usage of familial imagery recognizes that even though it is a divine trust the family frequently becomes a structure of destruction rather than a medium of grace, and that even at its best it never provides more than a pale and distorted reflection of the ways in which God acts toward his children.

When we recite the words of the Creed we acknowledge that we have been born again, that we are now enabled to claim another Father, and that we belong to a new family far more extensive than the one from which we came. Consequently, the self can no longer yield to the temptation to regard the old family with unqualified seriousness, as though it were the last great good in a universe in which God had abandoned everything else. As it is with baptism, so is it also with the Eucharist: part of the meaning of this reenactment of the family meal is that the bread and wine are offered for the forgiveness by parents of children's expectations that were childish in their unqualified magnitude, and for the forgiveness by children of their parents' inevitable disappointment of expectations that only God could fulfill.

If these comments upon the root metaphor of Christian

faith are correct, it is evident that the conventional assumption that the first article provides us with three attributes of God—that he is our Father and the Almighty and the Creator—requires serious revision. The primacy that the Creed awards to almightiness and creativeness seems strangely remote from the world of the Bible, where these apparently cosmological attributions are subordinated to such other refrains as the righteousness and faithfulness of God, which are far more crucial for the portrayal of him who is known first of all as the God of the Covenant. But the tension between Creed and Scripture vanishes when almightiness and creativity are understood neither as several predications chosen from among many possibilities, nor as sharing the same status as the affirmation that God is Father, but rather as explications of the meaning of this particular fatherliness. These two attributes are the differentia between God's triumphant fatherhood and all analogues to it within the world around us. Almightiness denotes the power of God to fulfill all his fatherly purposes and creativeness denotes the fatherliness of all the purposes that God fulfills. They are first disclosed to us together, not separately, in the gracious gift to the fractured self of the power to affirm the two initial words of the Creed, "I believe."

Although the notion of a root metaphor is immensely valuable for the interpretation of the Creed and of the totality of the Christian vision, it must be emphasized that the fatherhood of God is neither a dictate of common sense nor, indeed, a metaphor at all. This world which is the merest speck among the galaxies often seems alien and indifferent toward us, compounding the ravages of our predatory ways with ourselves, and in no way concerned to memorialize the ephemeral creatures who pass away as quickly as sparks fly upward in the night. Nature and history conspire to augment the burden of hunger and disease and death out of season. So we can scarcely begin with some ideal portrait of fatherhood and hope thereafter to discover that experience provides reasons to believe this is the most appropriate analogy for interpreting the ways of God. Frequently the best proof of the inventiveness of our kind seems to be our inexhaustible capacity to deceive ourselves. Experience counsels nothing unambiguous.

How is it possible, then, to confess that I believe? The Christian answer is that in Jesus Christ, his only Son, God reveals himself as Father, not only fatherly toward us but Father through all eternity. We become his children by adoption, but Jesus Christ is his Son forever. This disclosure means that all our notions of fatherhood are challenged and each is found wanting. But if the word can properly be predicated of God alone, how is it possible for us to understand what it means? The answer lies in the biblical narrative of Jesus Christ, which both justifies the attribution and furnishes our principles for its interpretation. The Creed does not need to speak independently of the mercy or righteousness or love of God, as though these were attributes alongside his fatherhood, for they are all comprehensively disclosed in the concreteness of his fatherliness when he comes to adopt us in his Son. (Parenthetically, it might be remarked that faith in God as Father has nothing whatsoever to do with dreary contemporary debates about masculinity, femininity, and sexism. God is the Father of Jesus Christ, which means that the universe is ultimately personal and therefore is an appropriate context for men and women together.)

A third topic that we must explore at least briefly concerns some of the implications of the root metaphor, and especially its significance for interpreting the image of the self as child of God, which is otherwise vulnerable to great distortion. There are two principal and deeply conflicting ways in which this master image has been employed in the West. In an unpublished work, Julian N. Hartt describes them in this way:

> The biblical form of this image makes much of human capacities for hearing and responding appropriately to God's creative and covenantal word. Nowhere in the Bible is a serious effort made to classify or categorize the being and powers of God and man under common concepts such as

reason, spirit, creativity, truth-capabilities, and moral passions. . . . Child of God in classical Greek philosophy represents man as endowed with a god-like power, Reason. By the proper exercise of this power man can be rightly related both to his own nature and to the ultimate divine cosmic structures.

The first article offers no warrant at all for interpreting child of God to signify that the self is related to the divine life because of its rational capacities or any other innate endowments. There is no suggestion of any affinities between creature and Creator. When the master image is seen in the light of the root metaphor that emerges from the biblical narrative to which the second article points, it displays a mysteriousness and complexity wholly absent from the hellenic model. *This* child prefers darkness rather than light, falsity instead of truth, and does what he does not want and does not do what he wants. The biblical image insists that the child is disobedient, that his reasoning is flawed, that he has become a prisoner of idols fashioned with his own hands but whose embrace he is powerless to break, and that he is afflicted with a strange and terrible hardening of the heart until he is healed by the gift of God's free grace.

The function of the image of the child of God is to render explicit our own involvement in the root metaphor and affirm that now God is our adopted Father as well as the Father of Jesus. When the accent falls upon the first word of this confession, *God* is our Father, persons find reason to cherish themselves even when all the reasons the world could offer have vanished. Because God is their Father, they are worthy to exist and worthy in existence; no worldly evidence against them can contradict the significance of this paternity. Beyond the thrill of the moment, beyond this cause or that appeal, beyond these communities or those values, there is God our Father, whose presence means that the world is stripped of its alleged divinity and denied its pretensions to be holy, righteous, and immutable. So the self is more than a reflection of the idols to which it has succumbed, more than all its worldly relationships, more than the sum of the functions it performs and the roles it plays. In this "more" there is always reason to honor oneself and reject the pretensions of the world to define the individual wholly in its own terms.

When the second word is stressed, God *is* our Father, we are asked to see the world not as dream or illusion but as a patrimony and home no less real than those to whom it has been given, for God is the source and sustainer of the actual as well as the ideal. On the other hand, beyond the world, God *is,* and so everything within the world is reduced to creaturely and human proportions, often formidable, sometimes terrifying, not infrequently stronger than ourselves, but creaturely nonetheless and therefore subject to the exercise of our freedom and invention. All else is humanized because God exists, and for this reason the self can muster the basic trust that creativeness presupposes. Faith in the living God demands no less than a sense of the worthwhileness of the self, of its strivings, and of the world bestowed upon it. We do not stand alone, without hope of help, in a land where enemies abound.

When the emphasis lies upon the third word, God is *our* Father, we affirm that we can find no fulfillment in this world or the next except in relation to others, and that for the sake of God these others must be cherished in all their otherness and distinction from ourselves. Every difference of age, nation, race, clan, and culture is relativized because of the gravity of the relationship that binds each to all. Because God is *our* Father, the neighbor is someone for whom the self is responsible, and not only the neighbor but also the stranger. All of us are children of God, summoned into existence for the sake of communion with the Father. Each of us is no more than *a* child of God, one among a multitude, not loved the less because he or she is only one among many but bound to all others because of this shared paternity, a tie that nothing in all the universe can nullify.

When the last word is the focus of attention, God is our *Father,* we have summarized the whole story, for this root metaphor that is meant to shape every facet of our vision and all our conduct points unfailingly toward the biblical narrative of the only Son, Jesus the Lord. Yet the metaphor is both more and less than a summary—more because it is far richer than every attempt to explicate its meaning, perhaps also less because the master image of selfhood that it offers to us, unlike the ones that idols afford, is limitlessly expansive and capable of development. In times of crisis, all of us regard whatever is precious and threatened as though it were, at least for the moment, the center of value. Nothing else seems to matter if only a parent is cured or a child healed or a business or valley restored. Then the crisis is past, and once more we can see the multitude of our responsibilities and the amplitude of our blessings in some reasonable perspective. But we can find no perspective upon our relationship to God; we can only find perspective within it, a perspective upon all our other perspectives.

In good times and bad, in youth and old age, in joy and sadness, in strength and weakness, at work and play, *this* is the center of value, the spring of existence, the source of the image that rules all our more fragile imaginings of ourselves and our possibilities—in the beginning and in the end, *God the Father*. A sense of identity is fashioned from many images, of course, not one alone. In human affairs, when all seem to fall away until only one remains, that is a prelude to sickness. But in the affairs of persons with God, the falling away of all except the *unum necessarium* is accompanied by the restoration of everything. That has been the claim of this chapter and is part of the miracle expressed by the mysterious words, "I believe."

3

"Almighty, Maker of All"

Root Qualifiers

The argument of the preceding pages was that the fatherhood of God is the root metaphor of Christian faith. It
furnishes the perspective from which everything else must
be seen and interpreted. Several subordinate claims were
also advanced in the context of the affirmation that God
becomes our Father by adoption because he is eternally the
Father of the only-begotten Son. The first claim was that
the master image of child of God is not only justified by the
root metaphor but also divested of serious ambiguities.
The second was that this image is more malleable and
expansive for self-understanding than all the imagery derived from the idols we inevitably create in our flight from
the true God. The third claim was that the first article does
not affirm of God three more or less equally significant
predicates. The attributes of almightiness and creativity
are the differentia of this particular fatherhood, qualifiers
of it and not independent affirmations that stand beside it.

Nowhere in the Creed is attention directed to the question: *How?* How is this planet sustained in the icy vastness
of space? How is it that there is something and not
nothing? How is it that this something does not subside
into nothingness again? From the perspective of Christian
faith, the point of departure can scarcely be "the ineluc-
table modality of the visible" and all the puzzles it presents,
but only the sovereign and gracious presence met through
Jesus Christ amid all the clutter, wonder, and irritations of
the everyday. *Who* is he, who constrains us to recognize
that he is not only one among many but Alpha and Omega,
the First and the Last? He is the Father, a Father so different that we must ascribe almightiness and creativeness

to him in order to acknowledge his otherness from all parents of whom we have hitherto heard. Only because we know *who* he is can we confidently address our first topic and answer the question of *why* it is that the world exists.

A perennial response to the question of the origins of the universe has been the myth of a demiurge, such as the deity of Plato's *Timaeus.* The myth portrays God confronting a material realm that shares his eternity but reflects nothing of his perfection. God endows the wilderness with the measure of order to which it is amenable, so that it gains a certain splendor and beauty that it would not otherwise possess. Whatever pain and darkness afflict the world are reflections of its original independence; whatever fulfillment can be found therein testifies to the benevolence and intervention of the divine. The allure of the myth arises from the power with which it can address not one question but two: the mysteries of suffering and of the existence of the world beside a God who is perfectly rich and complete in himself. But it finds no resonances in the Creed, for it betrays the root metaphor and reverts from the question of who is met in Jesus Christ to a query about how everything began.

Among the implications of the root metaphor that it contradicts, none is more fundamental than our conviction that *creation is grace.* We are enabled to claim that God is our Father only because "God was in Christ, reconciling the world unto himself" (2 Cor. 5:19 KJV). Reconciliation is the highest form of God's creativity that we ever encounter, and so it furnishes a paradigm for the interpretation of every other instance. Consequently, creation must be understood as an act of grace. Although it is possible to discriminate between his creative and redemptive operations, nature is itself the effect of grace and testifies along with the history of redemption to the limitless reaches of the love of the triune God. That we may exist, that others may also exist, that we may exist for and with one another, that we may will, that we may will together, that we may do something but need not do everything and sometimes may do nothing at all—how else could we speak of this except as the grace of him who, needing nothing, yet wills there should be what is other than himself and gives it a season of its own?

The Christian tradition has said that the world exists in order to reflect and bear witness to God's majesty, beauty, righteousness, and grace—in order to be the theater of his glory. As human artifacts express the craft and personality of their makers, so does the whole world testify to the sovereign creativity of God. How could it be otherwise? How could the universe be less than wonderful, when it comes to us from his hands? How could the intricacies and beauties and inherent intelligibilities of the creation not elicit our bedazzled thanksgiving, when severally and together they point to the glory of God? From every side, the natural order praises him

> who hast stretched out the heavens like a tent,
>   who hast laid the beams of thy chambers on the waters,
> who makest the clouds thy chariot,
>   who ridest on the wings of the wind,
> who makest the winds thy messengers,
>   fire and flame thy ministers.
>
> (Ps. 104:2–4)

But fidelity to the root metaphor demands that creation be understood as more than simply a display of God's power and glory. The world is an expression of the glory of the *Father* who, as Luther tells us, created it from "sheer fatherly kindness and compassion." God wills what is other than and distinct from himself, not merely a replication or reflection or shadow of his own reality. He does not repeat himself in some radically diminished mode, but summons into existence creatures who are entirely different. Ungrudgingly, he offers to them the full measure of liberty appropriate to their natures. So that they might exercise all their own creativeness, he establishes a world that is neither illusory nor immutable, for then it would offer no possibilities for finite inventiveness, but rather is responsive to the exercise of their agency. The creature, awarded its own liberty, is permitted and encouraged to become a creator, not a rival of the Creator but genuinely innovative because fashioned by the Father's love.

Because the world, for our sake, has been endowed with its own contingent reality, the decisions we make within the structures of time and space are frequently irreversible and the losses incurred therein often irretrievable. But this certainly does not mean that the world has been left to its own devices and allowed to become independent. Creation is *creatio continuata:* yesterday, today, and always, the world depends wholly upon God for its existence and all its possibilities. Without God, nothing: this is the formula for tomorrow as much as for the first day of creation. Because the universe was made *ex nihilo,* there was never anything beside God except what God willed to be there, never anything that contained its own independent principle of existence, never anything at all apart from the sustaining power of Father, Son, and Spirit. Consequently, we are set at liberty in an environment that has been fashioned wholly to our own measure, in order to exercise our powers of invention so that the realm of the actual might be enriched and expanded not only by the unfailing operations of the Supremely Actual, but also by the works of all the actualities whom God has made.

The fatherly glory of God is revealed in the unforced creativity, the spontaneous initiative, and the productive innovation of what otherwise would never be, by the creatures whom he has summoned into existence and wills to adopt as his children. Their liberty is real only because it is the product of his perfect freedom, but its derivation from his in no way whatsoever jeopardizes its character as liberty. The self has potentialities that can be realized by no agency except its own, not even by those others who love it most: "No father can be a man for his son, no mother a woman for her daughter" (William F. May [Northampton, Mass.: *The Daily Sophian,* April 1966]), and this is true even in the instance of God the Father. There is some value, perhaps, in an often cited aesthetic analogy. The characters whom a writer invents swiftly assume a considerable measure of independence, so that they cannot be manipulated arbitrarily but must be allowed to speak and act in ways faithful to their own natures. But this appropriate speaking and behavior are possible only through the instrumentality of the author, whose art remains the source and assurance of all their freedom and agency. The limitation of the analogy, of course, is that the human act is done only once while the divine is always necessary. The world, therefore, is properly understood as a theater for the expression of the glory of God the Father, and nowhere is this more fully manifest than in his children's fulfillment of the potential that is, wholly by his generosity, truly their own.

The creaturely potential, the human liberty, and the worldly context for their employment are all gifts that God lavishes upon us. But we are free to throw away our freedom. The story of the tower of Babel insists that human invention is never more inventive than in the fashioning of idols or in the idolatry of inventiveness itself, as freedom is everywhere squandered to sell the creature into new forms of bondage. The testimony of the world to the glory of God is not effaced by this rebellion, but we can no longer decipher its significance. All the eloquence with which the world points to the Father goes for nothing, unless the eyes and ears of the sinner are opened by God's disclosure of himself in Jesus Christ. Because the fallen world still has him for its author, however, people cannot live neutrally within it or act neutrally toward it. When hearts are darkened and all knowledge of the true God is lost, people will make gods of themselves or for themselves, and these daimons will haunt the human commonwealth and forever set this house against itself. So there emerges within the world a realm of illusion that veils and distorts all the contours of reality.

The power these spurious divinities exert is vast, but it is power rooted in illusion and therefore vanishes like smoke before the winds of a storm when people are confronted with the presence of him who is the source and ruler of all. Apart from his reconciling initiative, however, there is no remedy for the conspiracy between our passion to surrender to something greater than ourselves and the now enigmatic testimony of the world to something beyond itself. Because the freedom that God has conferred upon his creatures is utterly genuine, it is always unstable and can be conserved only by God's own involvement in human affairs. Our relative independence of the world and our absolute dependence upon him are indissolubly bound up with each other. Only because God is free for his creatures can they be freed from what they do to themselves and liberated for creativity again. This restoration of freedom through the miracle of reconciliation discloses to us his almightiness and creativeness, and the meaning of these attributes is the topic that we must now explore.

The attribution of almightiness is an indispensable clarification of the concrete fatherliness that we encounter through Jesus Christ: it denotes the perfect correlation of God's power and his fatherly design. The Father of Jesus is distinguished from all others because he is not a father who can do anything at all but the one Father who does nothing that does not perfectly implement his fatherly will. Almightiness does not mean that God is sovereign and omnipotent in some abstract sense. Rather, it means that he is triumphant *in* his fatherliness, not in addition to it or apart from it, as though he possessed some other nature or will than that which is revealed in the eternal Son. His acts are bound by his being, his being is expressed in his acts, and there is no shadow of inconsistency in the fatherly nature that is disclosed to us through the work of Jesus Christ. This predicate is not, therefore, an adumbration of or reference to perfections that some allegedly "natural" notion of God might seem to imply. There are no reasons to approach the first article as though it could be interpreted in terms of what is known independently of the Creed and the biblical narrative.

When Job asks God to explain the reasons for his loneliness and pain, the Lord more than matches the question with one of his own:

> "Where were you when I laid the foundation of the
>   earth? . . .
> Or who shut in the sea with doors,
>   when it burst forth from the womb;
> when I made clouds its garment,
>   and thick darkness its swaddling band,
> and prescribed bounds for it,
>   and set bars and doors,
> and said, 'Thus far shall you come, and no farther,
>   and here shall your proud waves be stayed'?"
>
> (Job 38:4, 8–11)

In theological perspective, however, there is more of almightiness disclosed in bringing sinners to repent, fugitives to return, enemies to community, and prisoners to freedom, than even in the laying of the foundations of the earth, for persons have what the earth does not—their own inalienable powers of agency and choice. If we are properly to understand the almightiness of God, we must remain within the clause where it is affirmed: the evidence that God is omnipotent and creative appears first of all in the words "I believe."

This is a confession by persons who know themselves to have been strangers and enemies. They did not choose but were chosen; they did not seek but were found. In this act of unfathomable grace, the almightiness and creativity of God are together disclosed, for what is harder than the stony hardness of the human heart or more creative than the work of reconciliation? "I believe" can be said only by those who have been constrained to admit the magnitude of their sickness, who have sorrowed for what they have been and done, and who have recognized the justice of the judgment that has been pronounced upon them. Their adoption as children is inseparable from their acceptance of the righteousness of this condemnation, an acknowledgment implied by the words with which they point away from themselves toward him who is the instrument of forgiveness and agent of reconciliation: "I, yet not I, but Christ in me." Forgiveness is nothing more than indifference or forgetfulness apart from the recognition of fault, and judgment is rarely constructive if it is severed from forgiveness.

Judgment, repentance, and forgiveness are the elements of reconciliation, which means the reunion of what has become separated or the mending of what has been broken. But it is far more than the restoration of an original situation. The ruptured relationship gains new dimensions when it is restored, for now it incorporates the admission of fault, the reaffirmation of order despite the magnitude of its cost, the overcoming of disappointment and pain, the disavowal of the desire for recompense, the courage to risk the self again, and the determination to live toward the future rather than from the past and thus transform failure into victory. No inventiveness in the world of artifacts rivals the richness of the creativity expressed in this renewal of personal relationships, which are the greatest goods we know.

The introductory words of the Creed, therefore, prepare the way for the remainder of the first article by providing a preliminary warrant for affirming the *root qualifiers* of almightiness and creativeness as the differentia of the fatherhood of God. They are root qualifiers because they function as adjectival explications of the root metaphor that are indispensable if it is to be adequately understood. It is only the narrative of Jesus which demonstrates beyond question that God must be acknowledged as Creator, because it is from this story of the divine act of reconciliation that we learn of God's power to fulfill all his fatherly purposes and of the fatherliness of all the purposes he fulfills. But the introductory confession also supports the attribution, for this "I believe" expresses the effects of that divine operation.

There is nothing so impenetrable as the hardness of the human heart and nothing so difficult to mold until it contributes to the fulfillment of God's fatherly design as the stubborn citadel of personality, filled with all its resentments and disappointments, its anxieties and animosities, with the sour taste of its guilt and the burden of pretensions of which it cannot entirely persuade even itself. If the grace of God can strike like lightning into this obscure terrain of the heart, illuminating and transforming and rendering suddenly fertile all the stony landscape there, then is it not proper, is it not necessary, to affirm that he is Creator of all?

As our final topic, we must show why it is wrong to allege that the root metaphor and the master image of the self conspire to enforce upon us an immature dependence inappropriate for "a world come of age." Nowhere except in the story of the Crucified can the meaning of *Father* and *child* be clarified. The christological reference of the master image strips it of any suggestion of immaturity, for this filial relationship is perfected only because Jesus "did not count equality with God a thing to be grasped, but emptied himself . . . humbled himself and became obedient unto death, even death on a cross" (Phil. 2:6–8). The biblical narrative insists upon the parallel between this history into which we are incorporated and the history of the exodus, when the people of God were first brought forth from captivity and set free in order to tame a wilderness where rich opportunities demanded every resource they could find in themselves, if they were to flourish in a land where giants roamed and cities were fortified up to heaven.

We have argued that reconciliation implies the perfect fatherliness of *all* God's purposiveness toward his adopted children. Only from some perspective utterly remote from Christian faith, therefore, is it possible to ask whether the almightiness of God does not confront the creature as threat rather than promise, or whether his omnipotence does not at least potentially deny the creature a place truly its own where it is free to realize its own possibilities. The first article does not recognize the absurd notion of such conflict. We have argued that the creature is free only because God is free for the creature. The creature remains free only because God exercises his freedom constantly to restore to it what the creature itself has squandered. How could these liberties ever be in conflict, as though the liberty of the divine might somehow render the liberty of the creature illusory instead of conserving and renewing it? The root qualifiers that denote his freedom to be perfectly and always our Father mean that even our betrayals and disloyalties are employed within his design, as we are reconciled not only to him but through him to one another. His freedom is expressed, therefore, to challenge ours with all the new possibilities that inexhaustibly greater community affords.

The claim of the last lecture that the master image of child of God is more expansive and suggestive than all the imagery derived from our idolatries furnishes another perspective upon the issue. A master image is intended to control other images and suggest additional ones, reconciling and integrating the variety without reducing them simply to tedious reflections of itself. Among these, one that is demanded and directly implied by the image of the child is a representation of the self as inheritor. Every child possesses an inheritance: for some it is a patrimony of wealth or land, for others no more than a social legacy of language and custom; sometimes it is little more than a collection of physical traits. But no child lacks some inheritance, and so a Christian master image requires a complementary representation of the creature as an inheritor because it is an adopted child.

According to the Genesis story, selves are called to subdue the earth and exercise dominion over it. The taming of creation involves the promise to serve God with gratitude and to exercise responsibility wisely and not wastefully. Perhaps the representation of the self as *deputy* is appropriate, for a deputy acts authoritatively for a principal, although the authority is not his own but is derived from a relationship and the fidelity with which it is maintained. This figure captures the contingency of the dominion granted to the self; it can be revoked, for the world is given to us only as a commission and a trust. The child who serves as a deputy remains always a child of God the Father, but now an element of accountability and an appeal for inventiveness have been emphasized by the inclusion of a command and obedience model of selfhood within the gospel of our adoption. Some portrayal like this, at least, is necessary to explicate the master image in the light of the whole narrative of the covenant that is fulfilled and interpreted by Jesus Christ. Only a superficial examination of the familial imagery of Christian faith could support the contention that it enforces immature dependence—although a sense of dependence, surely, is not merely childish but also the final wisdom that age and experience counsel. In its own way, even the image of the child implies that the world is the theater of the Father's glory most especially as creaturely inheritors offer their own contributions to the realm of the actual and, thereby, display the grace of him by whom they have been called to wrestle with their own challenges and have been permitted their own time and space.

Parenthetically, it should be noted that in its developed Latin form the Creed affirms that God is Creator *of heaven and earth*. The words must not be construed as though Creed or Bible offered a picture of the universe. The Scriptures actually offer scraps of very different pictures because they narrate the history of God's covenant with his people and reflect little interest in a world view. The relation of heaven and earth must be understood in serial or historical rather than spatial or pictorial terms; these words do not designate two places within the universe, but rather the twin aspects of the careers that God has willed for his children. Our histories in this world are concluded by death; our heavenly histories begin when death has done its work. Death is the line of demarcation between them.

On the one hand, death is the appropriate culmination of life in this world, for its imminence affords life much of its savor and urgency; beauty is all the greater because of its ephemerality, opportunities more exciting because they will never be met again. On the other, it is a penalty, the consequence of our insane ambition to be like God, appearing as an enemy because of our intemperate ambitions, our anxieties, and our ineradicable sense of guilt. But the Creed avows that, as Creator of heaven and earth, God is also Lord of the line of demarcation between them. Death is not his enemy but a servant and instrument, and therefore not only a conclusion but also a commencement and a gift—though not because of anything latent in the creature itself. On the contrary, death stands in the wings mocking every human pretension to lordship, testifying there is finally no sovereignty either in heaven or on earth except that of him who alone can effectively tame and master death and use its power as his own.

The next words of the Creed introduce another article and fresh topics, but they also redirect us to what really precedes the first article and constitutes its presupposition—unless there are two different Christian messages, or else a Christian message that is no more than an appendage to the conclusions of a universal religious consciousness. Neither of these approaches, however, is congruent with the Reformed tradition. How can the self believe, except through Jesus Christ? How can it believe in an almighty Creator, except through him by whom reconciliation is achieved? How, except in the light of the cross, could it believe that even "If I take the wings of the morning and dwell in the uttermost parts of the sea, even there thy hand shall lead me, and thy right hand shall hold me. If I say, 'Let only darkness cover me, and the light about me be night,' even the darkness is not dark to thee" (Ps. 139:9–12)? To him, then, in whom there is no darkness and before whom all the dark is swept away, Father, Son and Spirit, be all praise, power, glory, honor, and dominion, now and forever.

4

"And in Jesus Christ"

Heuristic Device

The contention of the last chapter was that creation is grace. Even more than in the starry heavens, the glory of God is displayed as persons fulfill the possibilities their Father has offered them; the world exists for the sake of this expression of creaturely liberty as a witness to God's generosity. His almightiness and creativity denote the perfect constancy and the constant perfection of his fatherliness even when his children shun his presence and abuse his gifts. The familial imagery of Christian faith, far from suggesting infantile dependence, points to the maturity and sense of responsibility required of persons who have learned to see themselves as the inheritors or contingent beneficiaries of his grace.

Now we must explore the second article and the sketch there of the biblical narrative of Jesus, which furnishes the grounds for these and all other Christian claims. As a preface to the story, however, it is necessary to examine the significance of the small word with which the article begins, for this commonplace conjunction enshrines as many complexities as the pronoun that introduces the English version of the first article. Anyone who understands the meaning of "and" understands the core of the Creed; anyone who does not, comprehends little of it—although persons for whom it remains a mystery, we must remember, are often more faithful disciples than those who boast greater theological learning. So our initial topic must be this apparently unremarkable copula, this "and," about which four points are important.

First, it must be interpreted disjunctively; in other words, the subject of the second article is different from the subject of the first and they must never be confused. Whenever we are tempted to describe God by analogies to the unitary human self and its experience of its own internal diversity—its possession of irreducibly distinct powers in the exercise of each of which the whole self is active—we encounter the warning expressed by this disjunctive "and." We must not obscure the eternal triune richness within the unity of God. The Creed insists that Jesus Christ is not an avatar or a theophany, but a person forever distinct from the Father. Who is he? He is not the Father in disguise, but one whose humanness is neither illusory nor temporary nor irrelevant: the narrative of his resurrected humanity is part and parcel of the gospel—indeed, the heart of it.

Second, we have also emphasized the necessity to interpret this "and" conjunctively. The two subjects are no more independent of one another than the articles within which they appear: God is eternally the Father of the Son, and the Crucified is eternally the Son of the Father. They can never be separated; when they are not acknowledged together, neither is worshiped or glorified at all. Consequently, the attempt to describe God by analogies to a community of selves who share a common humanness is limited by the conjunctive aspect of the copula. We must not obscure the unitary life that is expressed in the triune richness of God. The Apostles' Creed insists there is no undisclosed divine intention hidden from us behind what is revealed in Jesus Christ. Who is he? He is God in the highest, sitting at the right hand of the Father. In him, therefore, the divine will is perfectly and forever made known.

Another argument is implied in this emphasis upon the correlative aspects of "and." The word is more than a copula, exercising the force of "because of" or "through," which denotes both the instrumentality of the Son and his own freedom. So the third significance of the conjunction is its implication that revelation and reconciliation occur through the Son because he is the instrument of the Father. The initiative is always that of the Father who sends the Son, and to whom the Son is steadfastly obedient. The cross of Jesus might retain much significance, senti-mental or otherwise, but it would not mean reconciliation unless the Father were present in Jesus Christ. The Son is not an intermediary, someone who by his own efforts reconciles to each other two alienated parties who formerly had no desire for the restoration of their relationship. On the contrary, he is the Christ precisely because he humbles himself, obediently accepts the form of a servant, and faithfully serves as the Father's instrument. Through him are disclosed the mercy and grace of one who is other than himself.

Fourth and finally, the conjunction also points to the agency of Jesus, whose own initiative is no less real because it is exercised in response to that of the Father. It is his free act when the Son who is himself the judge stands in the place of the judged and, for their sake, accepts the judg-ment that is their proper reward. We come to believe in Jesus as the Christ because it is only and exclusively through the Son that we are enabled to believe at all. In order to express this yoking of instrumentality and agency, the early church spoke of the "interpenetration" of the activities of Father, Son, and Spirit in each of the great operations that are nonetheless ascribed primarily to one divine mode of being—creation to the Father, reconcilia-tion to the Son, and sanctification to the Spirit. Conse-quently, it was possible to emphasize that it is the Father who "was in Christ, reconciling the world to himself" (2 Cor. 5:19) and equally possible to affirm that "all things were created through [Christ] and for [Christ]" (Col. 1:16).

So the copula with which the second article begins, and which initially seems so ordinary and unremarkable, has both disjunctive and conjunctive aspects, and these com-plementary meanings are reflected in the extended signifi-cation of the word, which points both to the free agency of the Son and to the initiative of the Father whose design is fulfilled through the instrumentality of the one who is sent. Between the fatherly initiative and the filial freedom there is no conflict, only perfect congruence.

Jesus Christ: a name, a history, a narrative. Jesus is the Christ: the earliest Christian confession, the structure of every Christian creed, the sum and substance of the gospel. As Luther wrote, "Gospel means a story, the story of God's and David's Son . . . That's the gospel in a nutshell." "Christ" is the Greek translation of *Messiah,* which means "the anointed one." In the *Institutes of the Christian Religion,* John Calvin tells us that in order to understand the meaning of the word it is necessary to examine the roles of the three types of persons who were anointed in ancient Israel: prophets, priests, and kings. This is the second of our introductory topics: the doctrine of the threefold role of Christ, or *Triplex Munus.*

As we have said, neither Scripture nor Creed displays even a trace of interest in the question, how? How is it that our humanity has been united with divinity in him? How can these utterly different natures become one, or creaturely time be joined with the time of God? Instead, the truly theological question is, *Who* is he? Who *must* he be, yesterday and today and forever, in order to have done what he has done for us and for our salvation? We must proceed from his work to his person, for we know Jesus Christ if we know his benefits. These benefits affirm the truth of the way that Athanasius answered the question in the fourth century: only if he is divine can he offer redemption, and only if he is human can he communicate it to us. The sketch of the biblical narrative in the second article reaffirms the divinity expressed by the conjunctive "and" and tells of its indissoluble union with humanity. But the story most insistently stresses his humanness, because even before his name is mentioned Jesus Christ has already been encountered as the agent of the great divine works of revelation, reconciliation, and redemption—else the first article itself could not have been affirmed. Who is he? He is Emmanuel, God in the highest, God with us and for us, God become like us and one of us, but without sin.

The *Triplex Munus* asserts that Jesus, as prophet, is the agent of revelation; as priest, the architect of reconciliation; as king, the one through whom our redemption from the world is achieved. Without presupposing abstract notions of humanity or divinity, the doctrine rigorously implies the truth of Athanasius's dictum. Like the prophets before him, this man brings a word from the Lord. Their words were contingent and temporary, however, spoken for a particular community and its particular situation. His word is unconditional, everlasting, and cosmic in its significance. So Jesus is not only the greatest but the last of the prophets, for there is no further word to speak. The discontinuities are all the greater because the authority of his predecessors was derived from a word they were given and which was often far different than the words they would have chosen for themselves. But he brings a message that is inseparable from his own identity. His words and deeds are invested with their decisive significance because they reflect the mystery of this presence in which God himself has come among his own to reveal his relentless and unfathomable love.

It is the priestly role of Jesus that is most crucial, however, for the reconciliation that he effects is not only the *prius* of redemption but also the site of revelation: it is in the death and resurrection of the Son that the Father is disclosed. The sacrifices offered by the priestly tradition were of limited and temporary validity, but the sacrifice of Christ is of unlimited and everlasting import. So Jesus is the last as well as the greatest of priests; beside his offering, all other sacrifices are gratuitous. "If the blood of bulls and of goats . . . sanctifieth to the purifying of the flesh; How much more shall the blood of Christ, who through the eternal Spirit offered himself without spot to God, purge your conscience from dead works to serve the living God?" (Heb. 9:13–14 KJV). In the Old Testament cultus, the priest offered sacrifices not only for the people but also for his own uncleanness, and the sacrifice was itself something given by the people to their priest. In this instance, however, the priest does not sacrifice for himself but is himself the sacrifice for others. Because the priest is wholly without sin, the sacrifice is made entirely in behalf of the people and all its benefits accrue to them.

In the New Testament, the atonement is described in different ways that utilize familial and juridical as well as cultic language and imagery. But no matter how it is portrayed, at its center there is always an exchange: Jesus stands in our place and he does this for our sake. He renders himself helpless in order to help the helplessness of those who can do nothing for themselves before God. In his assumption of our powerlessness his power is disclosed, for its consequence is the assumption of those who have been strangers and enemies into his place so they can stand with him before the Father. The judge is himself judged in the place of the guilty, in order that God might triumph over guilt forever. This exchange that all the great biblical interpretations of the priestly work of Christ in some way affirm is the ultimate justification of the claim that God is love.

Finally, the prophet and priest is also king. Unlike the kings of Israel, however, his dominion extends as far as the boundaries of all that God has made, unlimited in time and space, and from it no creaturely reality is exempt. It embraces death as well as life, the realm of the secular as much as the precincts of the sacred. The kingship of Christ means that the world is an appropriate context for the odyssey of discipleship and a realm to be faced with the assumption of basic trust. Despite all that is formidable and frightening there, it is irrevocably his kingdom; its threats as well as its promises are all relativized and qualified by his everlasting reign. There are no reasons, least of all "religious" reasons, for abstention from the beauties, challenges, and irritations that voyages of discovery within it entail. On the contrary, just as his humiliation is the prelude to exaltation, his suffering and death the background of resurrection, and his exchange with sinners the preface to dominion without end, so is it true for us that the way down is the way up: it is through the density and detail of the finite and worldly that we approach God the Father, who has willed and made it all.

The doctrine of the *Triplex Munus* is no more than an earthen vessel, however. The work of Christ has an inexhaustible richness that can never be satisfactorily expressed in doctrinal form, and it becomes all the more elusive because it is first presented to us in a narrative that, like all stories, resists translation into tidy conceptual schemes. In a sense, therefore, this doctrine is a token of the poverty of every doctrine. But it also seems to have its own singular problems. In its representation of Jesus as last and greatest of the prophets, it stresses his role as revealer of God without seriously addressing the importance of his disclosure of what it means to be human. But selves created to exist only in grateful relation to God can know neither their own true natures nor possibilities nor even the magnitude of their disobedience when by their own hand they have lost all knowledge of their Creator.

In its portrayal of the priesthood of Jesus, the great assertion that for our sake he has stood in our place is scarcely balanced by complementary attention to the claims that in some mysterious fashion we now stand in his and that our old selves have been put to death by our baptism into his crucifixion. In its affirmation of the kingship of Christ, its focus upon the present reality and universal extent of his dominion can minimize the tasks and perils that still confront us, unless equal attention is paid to the hiddenness and futurity that also characterize his reign and thereby invest every dimension of the Christian vision with a thoroughly eschatological cast. Furthermore, these themes that receive least attention are the ones that would appear most important if, in fact, the Creed is an identity avowal. Therefore, especially in the light of our claims in behalf of the particular rather than the general and imagery instead of concepts, why should this *doctrine* occupy so prominent a place as soon as the name of Jesus is spoken and even before his story is sketched in the Creed?

The question provides the final topic we must address and requires a threefold answer. First, we have noted that a sense of selfhood is developed from and reflects our relationships with what is other than the self. So the emphasis properly lies first of all upon him to whom the self is related, not upon the state of its own subjectivity. We have argued that precisely *because* the Creed is an identity statement it directs our gaze steadily toward him from whom we now claim to derive our identity, not toward ourselves; it orients us toward the objective statement that the identity avowal presupposes and then sketches in the second article. So there is no tension between this interpretation of the Creed and the centrality we have awarded to the *Triplex Munus.*

Second, the doctrine expresses more systematically than the biblical narrative the latter's claim that Jesus Christ is a *concrete universal*—in other words, in and through him we gain a sense of identity not as a reflection of our own commitments but as an obedient acknowledgment of "the way things are." He *is* the center of everything, neither transformed into what he inherently is not by our loyalty nor rendered less than what he inherently is by our disobedience. In the Pauline letters, much attention is devoted to the parallel between two Adams, the old and the new. As a new Adam, Jesus is both *a* man and *man,* concrete and a universal. This is explicated by the *Triplex Munus,* which exhibits his power to incorporate us into himself in a way that sustains and is presupposed by our claim to discover our identity in him.

In his prophetic role, Jesus in his unsubstitutable particularity is himself the universally significant Word that he brings: "He who receives me receives him who sent me" (Matt. 10:40). In his kingly role, his reign is universal but never the rule of a mere universal, for it is "at the name of Jesus every knee should bow" (Phil. 2:10). In his reconciling work, we find in one form or another a pattern of exchange testifying that this incomparable particularity is in no way in tension with but is the absolute foundation of his cosmic and universal importance. As priest and sacrifice, the sinless Christ is able to offer himself wholly because he possesses himself wholly. He can wholly possess himself only because God is in Christ, so that his history embraces our own in such fashion that "if any man be in Christ, he is a new creature" (2 Cor. 5:17 KJV).

So this doctrine of the threefold work of Christ expresses the conjunction of universality and concreteness that is first acknowledged by the confession that Jesus is the Christ, then proclaimed in Paul's recognition of him as a new Adam, and definitively reaffirmed when the council of Chalcedon asserts in 451, with reference to the Eucharist, that *this flesh* is life-giving: for us all, Jesus is the way, the truth, and the life. The *Triplex Munus* insists that it is only in relation to this individual that all of us can discover who we are, whence we came, and whither we go. Jesus is *the* concrete universal in his own personal life, antecedent to and independent of the art of the biblical narrative or of any other story to persuade us of the potential of its characters to amplify our understanding of ourselves. Not only must we look beyond ourselves if we are to discover the sources of our sense of selfhood; we must look to *this* source and to no other if our sense of identity is to correspond with the truth of our situation.

The final part of the answer concerns the role this doctrine can play in relation to the whole biblical narrative and especially to the brief reminiscence of it in the Creed. We have noted that, simply because it is a doctrine, the *Triplex Munus* is innocent of the freight of nuances and ambiguities that narratives convey, and for this reason it is an inadequate instrument for expressing the richness of the biblical story. But this same untidiness renders narrative vulnerable to all sorts of interpretations and interpretations of interpretations, as the history of New Testament study demonstrates. The Bible does not dictate a particular way that it must be read. Consequently, nothing is more important than an appropriate heuristic device, which is simply a sort of compass, so that people will have some point of reference that gives orientation and perspective within the biblical story or summaries of it. The doctrine of the threefold role of Christ is an appropriate heuristic device for many reasons: it teaches us to progress from his work to his person and, in moving from the gifts to the Giver, to ask *who* he must be rather than *how* he has come to be. It answers the question as Athanasius does, affirming that only if he is perfectly human and fully divine could he do for us what he has done. So it represents him as a concrete universal—that is, his particularity is *itself* the ever-lasting decision of God for us and for our salvation.

The most important aspect of the *Triplex Munus* is its combination of the greatest possible element of formality with its concreteness. The formality appears because the doctrine is nothing more than an explication of the meaning of the name of the person whose story the New Testament tells. He is the Christ, the Messiah, the Anointed One. The *Triplex Munus* simply explains this name by means of assumptions derived from the Scriptures by those of his contemporaries who first applied it to him, originally wrote his story, and witnessed the ways in which his words and deeds changed the meaning of the title they had bestowed upon him. This systematic portrayal of the significance of his name provides a heuristic instrument that is neither imported from somewhere outside the story nor an imposition of order where none was previously apparent. The name can be predicated of him only in the light of his actual career, for the career involves not merely the disclosure that the name is appropriate but a radical transformation of its alleged meaning. So people who otherwise would have no guide for their journey within the biblical story and its credal summary are offered a heuristic device that is not bound up with cosmological and anthropological assumptions from other times and places.

In conclusion, a few words must be said of the distinction between hermeneutics and heuristics. The former designates the art of literary interpretation that develops principles for understanding the Bible. There are many hermeneutical possibilities, for the message of the New Testament must be proclaimed in different times and places and rendered intelligible for diverse cultures and linguistic groups. But a heuristic does not mandate particular principles of interpretation or depend upon some antecedently developed self-understanding; it simply furnishes a point of reference, a basic orientation or initial perspective within the story. Persons will bring their own understandings of themselves to the narrative, of course, if only to have them overthrown there, but this is not directly the concern of heuristics.

So heuristics can be described as more or less timeless, while hermeneutics always intends to be timely. The contrast is not meant to represent one as superior to the other, or to suggest that one can supplant the other, but only to insist upon their difference. The *Triplex Munus* is a crucial resource for approaching the story of Jesus and its summary in the Creed because it has greater formality than all possible alternatives, and therefore it harbors less potential for doing violence to the text in the course of finding some firm anchorage there. It can structure our freedom to grasp the narrative and focus our vision without binding us to any particular hermeneutical commitment. The richness of this story, beyond all others ever written, demands a heuristic device that will admit many and diverse interpretations, while at the same time excluding all that would disorient anew the persons to whom it has brought some measure of perspective.

Now it is time to enter more fully into the narrative itself, remembering that in the context in which the Creed is recited—the whole liturgical obedience of the Christian community, and especially baptism and the Eucharist—we meet the crucified and risen Christ as exile and king, Word and prophet, sacrifice and priest, on mornings set aside to proclaim his dominion over the entire realm of creation. He, who comes to us as one who serves, is Lord of all, to the glory of the Father.

5

"His Only Son, Our Lord, Who . . . Suffered"

Narrative Substance

The preceding chapter argued that the first word of this article must be understood both conjunctively and disjunctively. The ambiguity reflects the complexity of the relationship of the Father and the Son, who is the author of revelation and reconciliation, and yet also a servant sent by the Father as the instrument of the latter's sovereign will. The second and third topics were the meaning of the doctrine of the threefold role of Christ and its importance as a heuristic device that provides us with our initial orientation within the biblical story. On the one hand, it is nothing more than an explication of the name of Jesus Christ; on the other, it portrays him as a concrete universal whose particularity is itself the everlasting decision of God for us and our salvation. This doctrine brings further definition to the root metaphor and its twin qualifiers. Fatherliness, sovereignty, and creativity, as they are revealed in the words and deeds of Jesus, offer us no promise of freedom in this world from care or want, conflict or pain. They were the daily bread of the Christ and they will be ours, too, mingled with our satisfactions and joys, until the eschatological unveiling of him as universal King.

In this chapter and the next, we shall not explore separate topics; except for two excursuses intended to suggest twin images of selfhood that are indispensable complements to the representation of the individual as child of God, we shall simply explicate the credal summary of the New Testament narrative. No matter how differently it is understood, the Creed always remains a confession that the self has finally been freed from preoccupation with itself and enabled to see the splendid contours of reality that hitherto had been obscured by the heaviness with which the shadow of the sinful self fell upon them. Only as we grow ever more familiar with the richness of the story that it summarizes, can we better learn to see our own episodic careers in the light of the coherence this narrative provides, and therefore also learn better to act with the responsive consistency that is the meaning of the words, "Christian character."

"His only Son, our Lord." The significance of the two phrases is the same, but the accent differs. Because he is God, we must always obey him as Lord; because he is Lord, we must always worship him as God. The familial imagery is immediately qualified and interrupted by the motifs of command and obedience. Both phrases insist upon the irreducible distinction and yet unbreakable unity between Jesus and ourselves. "Only" introduces the distinction in the context of familial imagery that, because of our adoption through him, pertains also to ourselves. "Lord" reaffirms the distinction, but the adjective that qualifies it points to the fundamental and utterly incomparable relationship from which we derive our profoundest sense of who we are.

The first phrase, as the doctrine of the prophetic role of Jesus affirms, emphasizes the unsubstitutable importance of what is definite, particular, and concrete. The words and deeds of this individual and no other constitute the irrevocable decision of God in favor of his creation. The second phrase, as the doctrine of the kingly role of Christ asserts, tells of the cosmic and universal significance of the exchange wrought by the only Son. This is not a religious or moral affirmation, as though it were in any way contingent upon those who worship him or find inspiration in his example. We act as priests of the whole creation when we confess that he is Lord. Where these words are heard and proclaimed, they can never set brother against brother but only bind persons more closely to one another and to the earth that we are intended to share and use for the welfare of all.

In the end, it is not upon our power and inventiveness or upon our ideals and communities that everything depends, but upon the life of a single man. In worldly terms, that life was not a triumph but a humiliation, not a success but an utter and abject failure. Even in its own day, it attracted no great attention, for it occurred in a place of little significance and the persons whom it touched were not at all remarkable. Now the time and culture in which it transpired sometimes seem irretrievably remote from our own. The documents that provide us with all we know of him are very few and, quite apart from the question of the accuracy of their reports, even these offer us no more than a brief narrative of a part of his career. Those who confess his lordship today are still deprived of that acquaintance with him that even the most indifferent of his contemporaries enjoyed. His past is past, never to be made present again.

Nevertheless, the message of the Creed is beyond qualification or compromise: everything depends upon what was done at this time and in this place, because of the identity of him who is called Jesus Christ. Precisely because he was present then in a way in which he neither is nor ever will be present again, what was done then can never be repeated, supplanted, or surpassed. But he who was, also is now, and will come again; indeed, the fragile joys of the present and the promises of the future have their ultimate foundation in the certainty that he who is at the right hand of the Father and will come again as judge is none other than he who came among us two thousand years ago. So we must speak of Jesus in all three modes—as past, present, and still to come. The credal sketch of his past displays the way in which his lordship is perfected and disclosed through his role as a servant. The suffering and humiliation that he embraces bear witness to the exchange of incomparable magnitude that the doctrine of his priestly office describes, as he chooses to stand ever more unsubstitutably in our proper place so that we might finally be found in his.

"Conceived by the Holy Ghost." The beginning and end of the narrative are wholly congruent, for the tale of his con-

ception finds its correlate in the story of his ascension. Jesus Christ has no father except him who is forever the Father of the only Son. From the moment of its origination, the life of Jesus *is* Emmanuel, God with us, God in the highest bending to the lowest, God in his sovereign decision to be for and with his creatures despite their sin. Jesus does not become the Son of God as a reward for his perfect obedience; he is not filled with the Spirit and adopted into sonship at his baptism or on some other occasion. Were this the truth of the matter, the initiative would lie not with God but with ourselves. He is a man like all others, but his humanity is not antecedent to or independent of his divinity. He is inseparable from God; he is God in the highest. The meaning of his conception is that he is Son by nature, while we are the children of God only by adoption through him.

Precisely because he stands, almost unnoticeable, at the edge of the picture, we must be careful not to neglect Joseph. As the representative of our agency and inventiveness, the symbol of human accountability and power, the embodiment of the pride and defiance of those who are determined to be their own masters, Joseph is simply pushed aside. He has no part in this drama; it is the woman who occupies the center of the stage, the woman alone with the freedom of God. The man is unimportant, unable to influence the course of this history in which the nexus of cause and effect is completely and incomparably interrupted and set aside. No more than a spectator, Joseph represents the helplessness of every creature in the encounter with the holiness and righteousness of the living God—and, therefore, the helplessness to which the adopted son of Joseph submits when he stands in our place in order that we as well as Joseph might be adopted into the righteousness and reign of Joseph's adopted son.

"Born of the Virgin Mary." The eternal Son is perfectly united with humanness from the moment of conception. His life, wholly a consequence of the sovereign freedom and mercy of God, is entirely like ours, except for sin, for

he also is born of a woman. His humanity is complete and genuine, lacking nothing, in its indissoluble union with his divinity. Just as the powerlessness of Joseph before God represents the condition of each of us, so does the birth of the Savior point obscurely toward the way in which sinners will be redeemed, for already the exchange between himself and creatures has begun. He is one of several infants born in a particular Jewish household. God in the highest is born of a country girl and, like every child, differs at birth from the young of all other animals because of his complete dependence. Even birds are able to break out of their shells, but a newborn human can do nothing at all; its life is staked upon its unqualified and unqualifiable suffering of the initiative of others.

So it is with Jesus, except that this dependence is chosen and embraced in eternity as the prelude to his identification at Calvary with the situation of the sinner before God. The Son, whose whole life among us can be summarized as suffering, discloses his lordship in the passage from his infantile incapability to the powerlessness that is the wages of sin, when for our sake he stands in our place. In the suffering of the child there is the first obscure intimation of the suffering of the cross. Here, then, are Jesus and Joseph, adopted father and adopted son, never again to be separated, united in their shared powerlessness—the helplessness that dares not even cry out for the intervention of God and the helplessness that is the center of God's work of reconciliation, so freely offered to us, so dearly bought by him.

This is the heart of the infancy narratives, the beginning of the proof that, finally and in a way which for them is utterly unimaginable, what the scoffers say of him is true: "He saved others; himself he cannot save" (Matt. 27:42; Mark 15:31 KJV). Here is immeasurable condescension: God in the highest not only bone of our bone and flesh of our flesh, but by his own sovereign decision as helpless as those he comes to save. From the Creed we learn nothing more of his early years, but this suffices to prepare us for all the congruences that emerge as he turns his face toward Jerusalem. They begin with the crowded inn where no room can be found, which suggests his exilic life and final expulsion from every community by the ignominy of his death upon a cross.

Then Herod's massacre of children who might someday have voiced messianic pretensions points obliquely toward his messianic realization of countless new children of God by the power of his helplessness. His presentation in the temple as a child foreshadows his purifying of it when his adult mission is begun. His baptismal washing by John in the Jordan prefigures the expiatory washing of his adopted kin by water and blood at the cross. Before the sacrifice at Calvary, however, there is the cleansing of the feet of the disciples whom he knew would flee from him and Pilate's cleansing of his hands in order to disclaim responsibility for the events rushing ineluctably toward their climax. These washings, bound up with his betrayal by community and religious tradition and the rule of law, by friends and enemies and the indifferent crowd, are together held within the embrace of the greater baptisms from which God wills that no one should escape.

"*Suffered.*" Why is it that such an ordinary term should be chosen to comprehend the entirety of his career, from birth to death? For a moment we must leave the story in order to offer three comments on the meaning of the word. First, it must be distinguished from pain and sorrow. Pain is a sensation that sometimes afflicts all animals, but suffering involves the question of meaning and therefore is peculiarly human. Pain can be an ingredient in it but frequently is not, as in instances of betrayal by a companion or community. Neither can suffering be identified with sorrow. All of us have had occasion to respond thankfully after suffering the solicitude of a parent or friend. So it is reason for gratitude as well as for sadness; it suggests the enrichment of possibilities no less than their restriction, and the fulfillment of the self as much as the self's exploitation.

Second, this ambiguity means that the word is simply a neutral representation of a situation in which our opportunities are shaped for better and worse by the attitudes and actions of the people we meet. Suffering denotes the responsiveness and mutuality that characterize human life, which is always life together. The agency of the self can be neither developed nor sustained apart from the agency of others, whose initiative is so often necessary if we are to find our own. Our liberty would remain *terra incognita,* featureless and flat, were it not for others whose needs and inventiveness impinge upon us and invest our freedom with specific possibilities. The limits imposed by their proximity do not constitute the borders of individual existence but rather the leaven from which human life is made. Their agency can also diminish and conflict with our own, of course, but this is a subordinate truth, not primary. Only by suffering are we set free.

Third, the universality of suffering is not an accidental truth of the human situation, as though it were an unfortunate but inevitable consequence of the magnitude of our desires. The self is created as a sufferer and finds fulfillment only in suffering, for selfhood is an inherently relational affair. The primordial form of community, that of mother and child, discloses the enduring shape of personal existence; the fundamental unit of human life is "you and I" and never the self alone. In theological perspective, selves are sufferers because they are summoned into existence by a gracious Word and claimed in existence by the presence that dwells within the sovereign Word. They are called to be responsive everywhere and always to the will of God. In the Savior, humanness is definitively revealed as suffering; it means being for others and with them, in obedience to the Father.

These are not presuppositions alien to the narrative but elements within it that are indispensable for its proper interpretation and for understanding both Christ and ourselves. It is apparent, therefore, that from this common word and the most uncommon realization of its meaning in the history of Jesus, we must fashion an image of Christian selfhood that, while subordinate to the master image of the child of God, has an undisputed primacy next to it—the self as sufferer. As a heuristic device, the doctrine of the *Triplex Munus* insists that if the new image is to be consistent with the story it must convey the integral relationship between suffering and fulfillment, which is not only a dictate of ordinary experience but supremely disclosed in the priestly obedience of Jesus Christ.

What are the different strands of the story that must be untangled in order to understand all that he suffered under Pontius Pilate? First, he suffers at the hands of men. A few are drawn to him but even they fall away, and never were their numbers as great as his opponents. The incidents of the New Testament relentlessly disclose his failures in the face of those whom he called a "generation of vipers." There are the Pharisees and Sadducees and scribes, the rich young ruler who went away sorrowing, Peter's folly at Caesarea Philippi, James and John competing for preference in the kingdom of God, and the disciples asleep in Gethsemane. Then there are also the merchants and money changers in the temple, Caiaphas and his colleagues, Judas, the night of Peter's denials, Pilate, the governor's soldiers, the mob in Jerusalem and, finally, the impenitent thief—so many who have ears but do not hear, so many who have eyes but do not see.

Yet it is not from their misunderstanding or malevolence or mere human frailty that the intensity of his suffering arises, but from the incandescence of his love and the fact that he must suffer alone. There is no one to share it, no court of appeal, no friend or family whose presence can alleviate his burden, for he has left his own household in order to embrace the crowd that mocks his love. As he approaches the cross, Jesus is increasingly solitary, and so the suffering is exacerbated now because there are no worldly reasons whatsoever for hope. He is alone; all hope of help is past. The disgrace of the cross is final confirmation of the severance of every earthly tie. He who is the revelation that humanness means being for others and being with them stands where no one is with him or for him. But this abandonment, this absolute betrayal, this helplessness and incomparable loneliness—all are integral to the exchange that he effects.

Second, Jesus suffers the assaults of the powers of darkness. He cannot escape wrestling with the disorderliness of the creation that is the consequence of the creature's defiance and abandonment of its own delegated and proper vocation. This mode of suffering, adumbrated in all his encounters with those who plead for the restoration of health or renewal of life, is more apparent in the meeting with the Gadarene (Gerasene) daimoniac, more explicit still when he wrestles in the wilderness with the question of his vocation and later in his repudiation of Peter's plea that he should not go to Jerusalem. As an exorcist, Jesus is engaged in a struggle that has mysterious cosmic aspects. The conflict is all the more intense because, while the crowds demand signs to allay their disbelief, the daimons recognize his identity and therefore know how high are the stakes for which they play.

Third, Jesus suffers the wrath of God; he submits to the inescapable destiny of the sinner before the immutable righteousness and consuming holiness of the Father. Because all creatures have sought to go their own way, they now perceive the Creator as their enemy: his sovereignty seems a threat to their illusory liberty, his righteousness the antagonist of their pretensions to decency, and his glory the opponent of their pride. So, in their rebellion, they stand beneath the divine *No*—God's cancellation and negation of everything they have become, his attestation that their lives are finally meaningless and impossible, his decision that their future is to have no future. But it is Jesus who for our sake stands where this judgment is pronounced; it is Emmanuel who submits to the judgment passed against all others in order to bear it entirely and forever away.

He stands in perfect and unbreakable solidarity with

everything that he never was: "He hath made him to be sin for us, who knew no sin; that we might be made the righteousness of God in him" (2 Cor. 5:21 KJV). Precisely because he has united himself irrevocably with all of us, he must be deprived of companionship either human or divine. "My God, my God, why hast thou forsaken me?" (Mark 15:34). This is the core of the suffering: that he, unlike those for whom he suffers, should recognize his separation from God, should understand their disunity as the source of his agony, and yet should be unable to recapture it if he is to be obedient to the Father until the end. As his identification with mankind is consummated, it becomes ever more true that "he hath no form nor comeliness . . . there is no beauty that we should desire him" because now "the Lord hath laid on him the iniquity of us all" (Isa. 53:2, 6 KJV). God in the highest is now in the depths, all beauty erased, all glory gone.

Finally, Jesus suffers in the sense that he is wholly responsive to the Father's initiative. This, which has sometimes been called his "active" obedience, provides the reason for and value of all the other modes of suffering that have been termed his "passive" obedience. He is the instrument whose suffering discloses the everlasting decision of the Father; God's disposition is not made different because of Calvary but is there made known. So the suffering of the Christ discloses not only his separation from God but also the eternal unity of Father and Son. In this sacrifice we discover the final helplessness of the Son as the expression of the almightiness of his love, his loneliness as the climactic revelation of his will to be with and to be for our sinful world, and his disclosure of the relational character of our existence precisely in his apparent isolation from it all.

Now we must weave together these four strands we have distinguished. The first and second are together the *prius* of his suffering beneath the righteousness of the Father. The exchange is effective only because it is absolute. He who is made sin so that we might be made righteous in him must elicit the consummate attacks of evil in order that everything might be borne away forever—not only our defiance but also the opposition of all those elements within the cosmos that somehow augment the weight of loneliness and guilt and death. So it is fitting that he should be betrayed many times by the flawed rock on whom he intended to build his church, and that Judas should betray him by what appears to be a gesture of love. The cross would be provisional, liable to qualification and contradiction, had not his life exhausted every possibility of sin in the responses it provoked.

The third and fourth modes of suffering must also be explored together. Jesus suffers God's judgment because from the beginning of his career he is perfectly steadfast in his suffering of the Father's reconciling initiative. In their inseparability, these twin forms of suffering display the unity of God's righteousness and love. Because God is holy *love,* his forgiveness is entirely free, offered first to those whose need is greatest. Because he is *holy* love, his forgiveness involves a price that only he can pay. The suffering of Christ must never be confused with the absence of agency; this servant who is Lord exercises his own freedom in perfect responsiveness to the will of the Father and to the condition of those whom he comes to save. His passivity, as "he is brought as a lamb to the slaughter" (Isa. 53:7 KJV), is itself the disclosure of his sovereign power. God in the highest, bending so low: God in the highest, becoming one with all that defies him, so that the enemy might share his victory forever.

"Was crucified, dead, and buried." Now his lonely march from Bethlehem to Calvary is finished. From the beginning he has set his face toward Jerusalem; death comes not as the interruption of his projects but as the disclosure of their significance. He who is "despised and rejected of men" (Isa. 53:3 KJV) suffers the death reserved for the heathen; crucifixion means separation from God's covenant with Israel. It means that Jesus was "made a curse for us: for it is written, Cursed is every one that hangeth on

a tree" (Gal. 3:13 KJV). The one who proclaimed the nearness of God has now become a stranger to him, consigned to a distant place from which no one returns. But the divine righteousness is not only a consuming fire but also the sovereign determination to *set things right,* to fulfill the covenant that creatures have despised, misunderstood, and betrayed—and so God makes the curse his own.

There have been, of course, many interpretations of the cross, and they emphasize in different ways the awe and love that it elicits, its vindication of God's righteousness, its substitutionary elements, the import of its exemplary sacrifice, and the meaning of its victory over sin, darkness, and death. But the inexhaustible richness of the event continues to outreach every imagining of it and all attempts to express its meaning in conceptual form. Still, none would dispute that "Christ Jesus came into the world to save sinners" (1 Tim. 1:15), that "with his stripes we are healed" (Isa. 53:5), and that all of this is wholly the work of God and wholly the work of love.

Like his life, his death is humiliation, exile, failure. Yet the way in which the darkness of his career is occasionally illuminated by intimations of future triumph prepares us to approach Calvary only in the light of his resurrection. The events are indissolubly joined, but they are also irreducibly distinct. When the cross is isolated from Easter, the history of the Passion dissolves into allegedly timeless truths that express the inseparability of tragedy and the human condition. When the two are merged, the resurrection becomes nothing more than a mythic representation of the supposedly enduring significance of the cross. But this really divests the cross of its entire significance because, as Paul warns us, "if in this life only we have hope in Christ, we are of all men most miserable" (1 Cor. 15:19 KJV). Only in their unity and distinction do they express the gospel of our assumption of his place because he has stood in ours—God's descent and our elevation, the Son's humiliation and our exaltation, the lifting up of him upon a cross and the lifting up of us in him.

One of the many consonances within the New Testament is the parallel that Paul affirms between the burial of Jesus and our baptism: "Know ye not, that so many of us as were baptized into Jesus Christ were baptized into his death? Therefore we are buried with him by baptism into death: that like as Christ was raised up from the dead by the glory of the Father, even so we also should walk in newness of life" (Rom. 6:3–4 KJV). Burial is the final witness to his humanity, his solidarity with us, and therefore his subjection to the divine *No*. He becomes a victim of the irreversible terminations that characterize time under the curse. There is nothing to do with the sinner, except to hide him somewhere until not even memory can render him present again. So it has been done to us in him: the shame, guilt, and loneliness all buried with him, so that now the past is wholly past and the future is freed of its weight. Because we have been buried with him, the cross must never be seen except as acquittal as well as judgment, for he took upon himself our sins, "blotting out the handwriting of ordinances that was against us, which was contrary to us, and took it out of the way, nailing it to his cross" (Col. 2:14 KJV).

"Descended into hell." Those who debate whether these words describe an actual event in addition to Calvary have misunderstood their significance. Although they are a late addition to the Creed and have little explicit warrant in the New Testament, they are of fundamental importance because they not only reiterate the perfect identification of Christ with all our sufferings and separation from God, but also insist that even those who have not known Jesus may share in the benefits of his work. The Creed neither affirms universal salvation nor restricts salvation to those within the visible church. But it does state without any ambiguity that the work of Christ incorporates more people than simply those who affirm the Creed. This is congruent with our original argument that the Creed is primarily an identity avowal and therefore is not intentionally exclusive in the sense in which belief statements or

loyalty oaths might be construed to be. "Descended into hell" means that the events of the life of Christ reach out to embrace not only the children of those who witnessed them but also their ancestors, that Christ's work is the center of history and stretches out not only toward its consummation but also to its beginnings, and that perhaps we who confess the Creed can prepare his way not only to those who come after us but also to those who have gone before us. But this anticipates what must be said of the work of the Holy Spirit, and so we shall leave it for a later occasion. For the moment, there is only silence—silence and the cold and the dark, the worms and the damp, the earth pressing so close and hiding the sun. But the victim is victor, to the glory of God the Father Almighty, world without end.

6

"The Third Day . . . "

Narrative Form

"The third day he rose again from the dead." God in the highest, risen from the dead: life triumphing over the tomb, love disclosing itself as stronger than the grave, righteousness reigning over sin, peace and freedom supplanting the curse, forgiveness banishing guilt and shame. All this and more, not as dictates of logic or truths of experience, not as counsels of hope or imaginative interpretations of history, but announced and assured in the career of a particular man, Jesus of Nazareth, Emmanuel. There are two more or less independent traditions in the New Testament that constitute the Easter proclamation; one is the story of the empty tomb and the other, quite distinct from it, is the account of his appearances to the disciples. In different ways, both testify that the subject of the narrative continues to be the same Jesus of Nazareth who died and was buried. Paul's encounter on the way to Damascus is typical of all the appearance stories: "And he said, Who art thou, Lord? And the Lord said, I am Jesus whom thou persecutest" (Acts 9:5 KJV). It is the crucified who lives again. Although he is no longer known after the flesh, the risen one is this concrete individual in all his unsubstitutable particularity.

Only from the perspective of Easter does the jumble of his history reveal the symmetry and coherence that were indecipherable until its end. Not only were the intimations of triumph ambiguous in the midst of his earthly career but the most important of them were not recognizable at all, for there is no way except in the light of his resurrection to see God's help in his helplessness, his invincible power in his powerlessness, his solidarity with all creatures in his isolation from everyone at Calvary. The unity of these apparent antitheses lies not within the realm of logic but only in the life of this individual, and the unity is not revealed until the Father sets his seal of approval upon the whole completed history. Consequently, although it is proper to pursue Christology from "below"—that is, by examining the life of Jesus, his sense of mission and assumption of singular authority—this will never satisfactorily demonstrate that he is the Father's only Son. The approach from below represents a necessary and ineradicable Christian interest, but it cannot provide the foundation for everything else.

Retrospectively, however, not only does design emerge from the apparent disorder of his life; the resurrection also confronts us with its own unique inevitability. As the Fourth Gospel (KJV) insistently proclaims:

> He that believeth on the Son hath everlasting life [John 3:36]. As the Father hath life in himself, so hath he given to the Son to have life in himself [5:26]. I am the bread of life: he that cometh to me shall never hunger [6:35]. Come to me, that ye might have life [5:40]. Whoso eateth my flesh, and drinketh my blood, hath eternal life [6:54]. Before Abraham was, I am [8:58]. I lay down my life, that I might take it again [10:17]. I and my father are one . . . I am the resurrection and the life . . . whosoever liveth and believeth in me, shall never die [11:25–26].

We who have heard the words of Jesus himself and those that the community has ascribed to him *cannot* think of him as dead, cannot think of him at all except as victorious over death and everlasting Lord. As Hans W. Frei has written in *The Identity of Jesus Christ* ([Philadelphia: Fortress Press, 1967], p. 148), "Jesus defines life, he *is* life: How can he who constitutes the very definition of life be conceived of as the opposite of what he defines? To think him dead is the equivalent of not thinking of him at all. . . . Jesus lives as the one who cannot not live." He *must* be raised.

The great miracle, then, is not that he should rise from the dead, for he is God's eternal Son, but that we should be raised and exalted in him, that his life and righteousness and obedient responsiveness to the Father should become ours also. But so great is the gift offered by so great a giver, as Paul affirms when he proclaims that Jesus is a new Adam: "Now is Christ risen from the dead, and become the firstfruits of them that slept. For since by man came death, by man came also the resurrection of the dead. For as in Adam all die, even so in Christ shall all be made alive" (1 Cor. 15:20–22 KJV). God "hath put all things under his feet" (1 Cor. 15:27 KJV) and "delivered us from the power of darkness" (Col. 1:13 KJV) so that "he might gather together in one all things in Christ" (Eph. 1:10 KJV). The great miracle is that his resurrection should include the restoration of a fallen world where all our enemies are now disarmed, all their claims denied, and all our treaties of complicity with them annulled. The resurrection of Jesus promises a new heaven and earth and introduces a whole new age, for now the irreversibility of time under the curse has been overturned by the reality of reconciliation and forgiveness.

Nevertheless, even though the dominion of Christ is more certain than all the seeming certainties of everyday experience, it has yet to be fulfilled. Until he comes again to consummate and unveil his hidden reign, we shall know sorrow and pain that will prove no less burdensome because of the certitude of ultimate victory. The relationship between the times of his resurrection and ascension and of his second advent is not only one of concealment and disclosure, but also one of tension, struggle, and conflict. The future reality is not yet wholly realized, and part of the miracle of God's favor is that in the time between the times we are allowed to offer our own contributions to the fulfillment of his design. He awards us permission to undertake a mission and promises for it the gift of his Holy Spirit.

Now, however, we must turn from the substance of the narrative to comment briefly on its form and show the need for an additional Christian image of selfhood to complement those of sufferer and child of God. First, the self is the only creature that not only has a future but knows it has a future; its quest for intelligibility can finally be satisfied by nothing less than a sense of an ending. Some of our experience has a narrative quality of its own, but this is always vulnerable to accidents and interruptions. Consequently, we need stories that convey a sense of an ending which can invest our past and present with the meaning and coherence that would stubbornly refuse to disclose themselves if we had no patterns of interpretation except those the present affords.

Second, this sense of an ending can alter present patterns of both thought and action. Expectations for the future enable us to see the world differently: they award to present patience a new significance, endow present planning with new urgency, and invest present leisure with greater preciousness because there may be none tomorrow. They also teach us to act differently, for they persuade us to live "as if" and "as if not"—as if the future were already present and as if whatever presently resists the future actually were not. So what does not yet exist can sometimes prove more powerful than everything that does.

Third, between a story's beginning and its end there must be elements of both congruity and incongruity. Without the former, a narrative would merely display the random and accidental aspects of life and leave us with them. But the latter are even more important, for they are the source of the story's power to serve as a medium of disclosure. Were the ending not to occur in a way that falsifies conventional assumptions and expectations, we would learn nothing we have not always known. The rigidities of these assumptions and expectations mirror the ways in which we have learned to understand ourselves and our world. Their overthrow constrains us to revise our view of the self's nature and possibilities. The more powerfully a story contradicts the conventional rigidity of our expectations, the more profoundly it can challenge a previously established sense of identity.

In its radical reversal of every assumption concerning human nature and destiny, the incongruity within the biblical story renders it an instrument of disclosure that counsels us to repent and understand ourselves in a *wholly* new way. The story presents us with what we initially want to deny and about which we would prefer to remain deceived all our lives—that we are helpless and ungodly, enemies and strangers to God. It also tells us that now there has been done for us what we could never do for ourselves, that God sees us clothed in the righteousness of Christ, and that we have been made participants in his risen life. When we are enabled to confess that our true history and future are found only in the history and future of this individual who is also a universal, a new Adam, the credal summary of the narrative becomes an avowal of a new sense of identity, for our old assumptions have been wholly overthrown. This sense of selfhood now requires an additional image that will convey the eschatological orientation of the Christian vision, express the significance of this sense of an ending for existence today, and support the permission to live "as if . . . as if not" and contend against appearances while the reign of Christ remains hidden and the old self within us struggles still.

The essential incongruity of the New Testament story appears only with God's declaration of approval on the third day, when the Father ratifies the exchange consummated by his only Son. This now becomes the necessary presupposition of every satisfactory interpretation of the work of Christ. The incongruousness of the exchange unifies otherwise unconnected incidents of the story and establishes a series of congruences that would all dissolve apart from it, but which now emerge as the structural elements of the narrative. *Was conceived . . . ascended into heaven:* as the humanity we share with him is finally assumed into the richness of the divine life, so was it originally perfected in the context of the divinity of the eternal Son. *Was born . . . dead:* the freely embraced suffering of the newborn is a token and pledge of the suffering by which many are born anew. *Suffered* . . . *and sitteth on the right hand:* this suffering is not the termination but the goal of his career, for it is the disclosure of his unity with the Father and the revelation of his almightiness. *Was crucified* . . . *shall come to judge:* the judge who was judged in the place of the guilty will come to attest their acquittal and complete the setting right of everything begun at Calvary. *Buried* . . . *He rose again:* in the incandescence of the resurrection, burial is disclosed as pure grace. The old is gone, the new begun.

The affirmations of the second article, because they are the structural elements of a narrative, are far more important than propositional statements of belief or characterizations incidental to a loyalty oath. Beliefs must always be revised in the light of new knowledge, and characterizations of an object of loyalty can be abbreviated until further abridgment would hide the identity of the object. But the structural components of a story cannot be altered or abridged without a fundamental loss that distorts the whole. When they are subjected to revision, the actual existence of Jesus is untouched, of course, but our access to it is diminished. His life is not restricted to his story, but we have nothing else that can introduce us to it and enable us to see its continuation in the present as well as its shape in the past. The elements of the narrative, unlike the ingredients of belief statements and loyalty oaths, are individually more important and together more integrally related than modern rationalism has frequently realized.

"Ascended into heaven." The ascension does not describe the visible exaltation of the Son, but rather his withdrawal from our loveless history into the history of God's trinitarian love. Nor does it presuppose an antiquated picture of the universe. Heaven is not a place; the word simply denotes life in the immediate and unmediated presence of the Father. The story of the ascension reiterates the unassailable sovereignty of the Creator in relation to the creature. As the Son was hidden in earthly humiliation, so is he hidden again in his ascended glory: his lordship is

manifest not to those who choose to acknowledge it, but is evident in his own choice of those whom he enables to affirm it. But if the ascension means the cessation of his appearances, which have no parallel at all in the later history of the community, it is a beginning as much as a conclusion.

Just as the story of the conception tells that God condescends to unite himself with a creature, the tale of the ascension affirms the elevation of the creature to share forever in the life of God the Creator. Now our own humanity is, in Jesus Christ, at the right hand of the Father, a pledge and token of our future life in the kingdom of God. He who is bone of our bone and flesh of our flesh is the everlasting Lord, God in the highest. The most profound meaning of the ascension is precisely the opposite of what it initially appears to suggest: he has not left us behind, has not gone away from us, but has taken us with him, so that in him we are already at the right hand of God—and no power in all the universe can dislodge us from the support and shelter of this almighty hand.

This same point is expressed in a different way by the claim that the theological significance of the story lies in its clarification of the nature of the Easter event. It would be entirely wrong to approach the ascension as a mythological and therefore dispensable assertion derived from ancient stories of the descent and ascent of savior gods. When the resurrection and reign of Christ at the right hand of the Father are isolated from it, their own significance becomes doubtful and elusive. The reports of the ascension testify that the resurrection must be interpreted not only in the light of the appearance narratives but also with reference to the tradition of the empty tomb. Even though he was no longer known according to the flesh during the forty days after Easter, his presence then was such that his withdrawal to the Father could not be expressed except in the temporal and spatial language of our everyday experience of ourselves.

"And sitteth on the right hand of God the Father." This and

the following elements of the ending march into the present and on to the future. In this new time, now oriented toward the approaching end and no longer toward the failed beginning, there is one constant and unchallengeable certainty amidst all the ebb and flow of history: "All power is given unto me in heaven and in earth" (Matt. 28:18 KJV). No matter how vehemently his dominion may be disputed by those who wish to be their own lords, he reigns. As Calvin properly insists, the right hand of God does not denote a place but a function, which is the exercise of all the power and authority of the Father. Because there is no divine will beside or apart from that which is revealed in the earthly life of Jesus, the affirmation that he sits at the Father's right hand expresses the perfect coincidence of God's almightiness and grace. All power that is God's power is grace, for such is his disclosure in the Son.

His risen lordship always confronts us as gift and permission. It means that we are now permitted to turn away from the idols we have fabricated for ourselves; because Jesus has borne the consequences of our fallenness, the bondage we have inflicted upon ourselves no longer constitutes a penalty beyond remission. Because his lordship is hidden during the time between the times, however, it is difficult for us to live in the light of the permission, and so this gift is accompanied by a still greater gift that supports us in our frailty. He who sits at the right hand of the Father not only has interceded for us, but intercedes for us today and will do so until he returns as universal Judge. No matter what we do or leave undone, no matter how terribly we betray the brightness of our promise or the trust of family or friends, he is at the Father's right hand until the end of time, interceding in our behalf. There will never come a day when it is no longer true that "we have such a high priest, who is set on the right hand of the throne of the Majesty in the heavens; a minister of the sanctuary, and of the true tabernacle, which the Lord pitched, and not man" (Heb. 8:1–2 KJV).

He reigns, and now the integral relationship of suffering

and fulfillment is beyond dispute, for us as well as for him. In the great passage of Philippians that speaks of the "self-emptying" of Jesus Christ (Phil. 2:5–11), it is said that the movement downward, the suffering, is causally generative of the movement upward, the exaltation. This does not mean that the lordship of the Servant can be construed as though it were a reward for his suffering, something merited but external. On the contrary, we have seen that it is only in his role as servant that his lordship is perfected and revealed. For Creator as well as creature, the expression of love is love's enrichment and the fulfillment of the lover. The infinite divine benevolence disclosed in his suffering finds its satisfaction not in the vision of future glory but precisely in spending itself for the reconciliation of the beloved. The life of Christ is the perfect demonstration that there is no fulfillment except by way of suffering: it displays the form of the human as being for and being with, in obedience to the Father. Only by suffering the Father's initiative can selves surmount the loneliness that is the wages of sin and be for and with one another again in a way that leads to their mutual realization of all their creaturely possibilities. Therefore, Christian faith claims that suffering is a synonym not only for the fallen human condition but specifically for the whole of redeemed existence.

"From thence he shall come to judge the quick and the dead." The once and future king who has come and now reigns will come again. Christian eschatology embraces not only the tension between present and future but also a constant reference to the past. The good news is that he who will come is the one who has come to bear all our sins away. The once and future judge is the one who has submitted to the judgment to which we were liable. That *he* will come to judge, then, is reason for unqualified hope, because yesterday and today and always he intercedes in our behalf at the right hand of the Father. This hope is all the greater because he who comes will come to *judge;* in the biblical tradition, as we have noted, judgment does not mean mere

punishment but the restoration of order, the setting right of a situation that has gone wrong.

Because Christian certitude concerning the future is firmly anchored in the past, it is entirely definite and not simply a vague expectation of the improvement of things sooner or later. But this concretion is combined with a significant element of indeterminacy, and neither is dispensable. If the ending were not concrete, it could not serve as a device for the interpretation of everything that precedes it and illuminate our contemporary situation. On the other hand, were it not also in some sense indeterminate, it would seem to render human resources unnecessary and to represent our world of possibilities as though its potential were already completely realized. The mixture of these two elements is evident in the Johannine affirmation that "it doth not yet appear what we shall be: but we know that, when he shall appear, we shall be like him" (1 John 3:2 KJV).

Because of its imminence and concreteness, the promised ending appeals to the self's own unpredictable liberty and creativeness to live "as if" and "as if not" in order to actualize possibilities in the present that not even God himself could realize in the mode appropriate to creaturely life. Existence in the likeness of the death and resurrection of Jesus Christ describes the constant attempt to render actual everything to which the "as if" points and to annul or reconcile all that the "as if not" comprehends; so it affirms the importance of every human resource, even though the ultimate realization of the likeness depends wholly upon powers other than our own. The permission to undertake a mission in the name of Jesus means that our history is not finally trivial, but has its own irreducible and unforeseeable contributions to offer to God's design.

Therefore, the end that has been disclosed has not been entirely disclosed, partly because in the time between the times it can be perfectly envisioned by God alone and, most important, partly because it is not a foreclosure of human freedom and inventiveness but an appeal for their exercise. So the great affirmations with which the narrative concludes will be misunderstood unless we recognize that they include God's permission of creaturely liberty and his determination to give the creature its own time, space, and delegated dominion. The enemies of God have been broken and defeated, but the struggle against them still requires unremitting vigilance; and in it there is an unsubstitutable place for the exercise of human agency and initiative.

The kingdom of those who reign with him shall have no end, as is made explicit in the Nicene Creed. Its duration will be utterly different from that of time under the curse, which is constantly interrupted by irreversible terminations that erase the features of whatever incipient design was there, despite all the passion and effort we expend on its preservation. On the other hand, its duration will also be entirely different from the apparent endlessness that often persuades us of the senselessness of the time between the times, in which there seems to be no point of orientation, nothing defined, little that can ever be illuminated by a cartographer's skill. Instead of featureless time that really offers neither time nor solace for us, there will be everlasting peace and joy. In the world without end, there will be the final verification of creation through Christ. So the end will return us to the beginning of everything, but now all will be incomparably and inexhaustibly richer than before.

The unity of the world lies not in itself but emerges as a consequence of our actions within it, for we have been delegated dominion over it. But our history has become an instrument of division, so that the world's unity remains unrealized. It is for this reason that creaturely apostasy is so terrible: not only has the self lost its own center but the cosmos has also been disfigured and deprived of the center it was ordained to have. Reconciliation in Jesus Christ means the setting right not only of the human situation but of the whole world; the embrace of humanity within the unitive power of the history of Jesus will unify the whole creation. The self will not be deprived of its world, for that is unimaginable, but will be granted it anew, fresh from the Father's hand. Then, in the kingdom without end, there will finally be realized the vision of the prophet Isaiah of a great day when "The eyes of the blind shall be opened, and the ears of the deaf shall be unstopped. Then shall the lame man leap as a hart, and the tongue of the dumb sing: for in the wilderness shall waters break out, and streams in the desert. And the parched ground shall become a pool, and the thirsty land springs of water" (Isa. 35:5–7 KJV).

These chapters on the substance of the story have contained two excursuses, one on the meaning of suffering and the other on the importance of narrative form. Narrative can satisfy our appetite for the sense of an ending that we need in order to illuminate the present age and orient our thought and action. This sense of an ending presupposes an element of incongruity that can overthrow conventional expectations and even a hitherto invulnerable sense of identity. Among the lessons we learn from the complete reversal of ordinary assumptions by the New Testament story is our need for an additional image of selfhood that will express the eschatological implications of the gospel and complement the figures of the self as sufferer and child of God. It is apparent that the light cast by this sense of an ending sweeps away images that arise in the obscurity of defeated time, the finally senseless imagery of the individual as prisoner and exile, stranger and victim. In life as in art, everything depends upon a sense of an ending that can identify the beginnings and resolve the paradoxes of our concrete histories—and that is to be found nowhere except in the resurrection and ascension of Jesus Christ, who reigns with the Father and the Holy Ghost, ever one God, world without end.

7

"And I Believe in the Holy Spirit . . . "

The Spirit's Role

The second article deals with God in relation to us, the third, with ourselves in relation to God. Their unity is evident in their mutual focus upon the exchange whereby Christ stands in our place so that through the Spirit we might stand in his. The first article provides us with the master image of our humanness: we are the adopted children of the eternal Father. The second recites the work because of which we are offered adoption, and the third tells of the actualization of adoption through the Spirit. So it is appropriate that the final article should begin with the reiteration of the words that constitute the Creed as an identity avowal, for now the reference to the Spirit and his works renders even more apparent the element of self-involvement that informs every line of the text.

The third article, no less than the first, is understood only when it is interpreted consistently in the light of the second. As the Father discloses his presence and agency to us only in the Son, so is the Son now present and active among us only through the Spirit. The Father draws near to us in the Son, who is present with us today by the Holy Spirit, who brings us through the Spirit to himself, and who presents us in himself to the Father. The spheres of Son and Spirit are identical: the latter bears witness to the dominion of the former and is distinguished from all the other voices in the world by the perfect consistency of his testimony to the risen Lord in whom the Father's sovereign love has been revealed. The Spirit has no work of which Christian theology is authorized to speak except that of bringing us into communion and community with the eternal Son.

And . . . the Holy Spirit. Like the copula that introduces the second article, this "and" is at the same time disjunctive and conjunctive; it affirms distinction as much as unity in God and subordination as well as equality. The biblical narrative insists that Son and Spirit are different and that, in some sense, the latter is subordinate to the former. The Spirit comes temporally after the Son; his role is to incorporate us into the work that Christ has antecedently accomplished once and for all. The Spirit is concerned with the subjective aspects of what is objectively complete, and he acts in the course of human history after Jesus is no longer bodily present with us but has ascended to sit at the Father's right hand. These distinctions between heavenly and earthly, objective and subjective, prior and posterior, are all expressed in the words of the Fourth Gospel: "It is expedient for you that I go away: for if I go not away, the Comforter will not come unto you; but if I depart, I will send him unto you. . . . He shall glorify me: for he shall receive of mine, and shall show it unto you" (John 16:7,14 KJV).

But equal attention must be devoted to the conjunctive significance of the "and." The Son who is the mediator of the Spirit that subsequently relates us to him is also portrayed in the gospel story as wholly directed by the same Spirit. The phrases "in Christ" and "in the Spirit" are synonyms because, after the ascension, the presence of one would be incomprehensible apart from the presence of the other. He through whom we hear the Word of God and by whom we are drawn within its orbit cannot be other than God himself. As Athanasius has written, "If the Holy Spirit were a creature, we would have no fellowship with God in him; in that case we would be connected with a creature and we would be alien to the divine nature, so that we in no sense would have fellowship with it" (Athanasius, *Letter to Serapion*, I, 27, *P.G.*). The early church expressed the complexity of the two introductory copulas by affirming that the Son is "begotten" while the Spirit "proceeds" from the Father and the Son together or from the Father through the Son. This language may seem opaque today, but its virtue is that the distinction drawn between Son and Spirit also serves to insist upon their unity, for it asserts that the immediate source of the eternal Spirit is the inner richness of the divine life. Furthermore, the Father, Son, and Spirit are equal in the sense that their discrete works are each the work of all; Father and Son are perfectly present in the operations of the Spirit, just as is the Spirit in theirs. So they are praised and glorified together.

Because the task of the Spirit is the completion of our adoption, the Holy Spirit means, first of all, *power* that is wholly different than our own. It is not mere force, however, but the expression of omnipotence as God's freedom to fulfill perfectly all his fatherly purposes. Therefore, the Spirit is *personal* power. Although he is formative of persons in ways that nothing less than what is inherently personal can be, the warrant for this assertion is simply his unbreakable linkage with Jesus. Only that which is itself personal can perfectly communicate the reality of personal presence, the companionship of the ascended Lord.

Third, the Spirit is *divine* personal power; as Athanasius understood, the Spirit could not be the agent of our redemption were he not one with the Redeemer himself. Finally, the Spirit is a *distinct* divine personal power. Just as the action of the Father in the Son is also the Son's own action, so is the action of the Son through the Spirit also the Spirit's own personal activity.

This form of God's presence constitutes an eternal mode of being of the one God, along with those of the Father and the Son. The early church recognized that it could proclaim nothing less than this if it were to speak of *revelation* at all. If we are concerned with more than our own perspectives upon a finally enigmatic universe, we must steadfastly insist that the Father's disclosure of himself in Jesus Christ, and the completion of our adoption through the Spirit, reveal God as he is in himself and remains forever.

Were this not true, the ultimate truth about God would still be hidden, in which case we would really have no gospel to proclaim and all speech of reconciliation and salvation would dissolve into finally uninteresting statements about ourselves and nothing else. In God, however, there can be no discrepancy between enacted intentions and identity. The Father's creativity and almightiness, the fatherliness of all his purposes and his freedom to fulfill them perfectly, provide the assurance that his nature, will, and activities coincide absolutely. God's being is revealed in his acts; his acts faithfully mirror his being.

The Holy Spirit frees and unites. He brings freedom because he enables us to recognize that everything Jesus Christ is and everything Jesus Christ does, Jesus is and does for us—so we need no longer try to be this or do this for ourselves, or look elsewhere than to our ascended Lord. The gift of freedom presupposes nothing in those to whom it is given except their unacknowledged need and the responsiveness that the Spirit himself creates. The story of the virgin birth, because of its unambiguous testimony to the uniqueness of Jesus Christ, asserts the radical contingency of the whole creation, and therefore of the new creation as well. So the virgin birth of Jesus points toward the freedom and sovereignty of the Spirit who comes after him, and attests to the unmerited character of an election that has no basis whatsoever except the inexhaustible mercy of the triune God.

Interpretations of the Holy Spirit have frequently erred because they have individualized or institutionalized his work, relating him primarily to the regeneration of the individual or to the powers of the ecclesiastical institution. But the first fails to recognize the communal form of personal existence, and the latter the primacy of the personal beyond everything else. Neither adequately expresses the centrality of the mission for the sake of which the community exists. The claim that the Spirit frees and unites is not without difficulties of its own, however, unless the meaning of freedom is concretely defined and the ways in which it is identical with unity are carefully explored. So we must briefly address three topics: freedom in time and space, freedom and law, and freedom in relation to others. The permission of our mission is a dominant refrain in them all.

First, our liberty is exercised in time and space; consequently, we must be able to speak of the renewal of these structures of human life if we are to affirm a new measure of freedom. Paul writes of our liberation from the disorderly creation that the first Adam was intended to rule but which now rules him and grows unruly because it has lost its steward—the disordered space in which we no longer have a proper place and the disordered time that appears endless and senseless because we do not know where it is going or, indeed, whether it is going anywhere at all. But as we are incorporated into the new Adam, these structures are transformed. Because we still live in the midst of the "not yet," however, we must employ our new freedom to complete the redemption of the lingering conditions whose oppressiveness is somehow related to our own disobedience.

We have seen how the biblical narrative affords us a new perspective upon the time between the times, because of the sense of an ending it provides in the resurrection of Jesus. Nevertheless, what is incomparably more important than the means by which we are enabled to see is the power that justifies the means, the presence of a new spirit among us now and forever, the Holy Spirit, God in the highest. Because the Spirit is himself the content of the future consummation, he is able to redeem time under the curse; no earthly power can finally contest his sovereign authority. He relates us to the Father primarily in horizontal rather than vertical terms, pointing not so much to what lies above us as to what lies in front of us. So the first words of this article direct us toward and complement its concluding assertions concerning the resurrection and life everlasting. But what lies in front of us is also with us now, for through the Spirit the risen and victorious Jesus Christ comes to strengthen us and assure us of the future unveiling of his universal reign.

No longer, then, can the time between the times be represented by either a circle or a line. Now time is oriented toward the consummation God has prepared for it and no longer circles back upon itself. Nor is it still characterized by irreversibility, for the reality of reconciliation and the presence of the Spirit unknot the cords by which the past has made us captive and promise the restoration of all that the curse has forced us to leave behind. But the great miracle is that now we ourselves become participants in the Spirit's cosmic work. We have said that the world does not find its unity in itself but gains it through the activity of those whom God has appointed as his deputies. As our histories are embraced within the reconciling history of Jesus, the restoration of the proper center of human life means also the unification of the world. Through the Holy Spirit, our lives contribute to a centered universe and we are enabled to exercise a priestly ministry toward it until he who is the ultimate center of both self and world comes again in all his glory and power.

Our disordered space is redeemed because the selves that exist in the new time created by the Spirit are granted permission to engage in his mission. Mission means that the self is placed. Our location is no longer a limit but an opportunity, not an accidental circumstance but integral to the narrative by which we are defined. The presence of others for whom Christ died and lives again anchors us in space more firmly than we could ever anchor ourselves. Their presence transforms space into a concrete determination of our capacities for responsiveness. Space as *placement*, not as something we can buy or sell or change at will, expresses the relational form of personal life: it means responsibility and accountability, and these offer us more freedom and fulfillment than we could ever find for ourselves.

Suffering the needs of others enriches our own possibilities and provides a focus for the exercise of powers that otherwise would remain unused. But we need to suffer those needs neither on our own terms nor on those set by others, but only in relation to righteousness, truth, justice, and love. The mission of the Holy Spirit means that not only is space humanized because it reflects the proper relationality of creaturely life, but it also becomes the context of the intersection of personal histories that enrich one another because they are together incorporated into the narrative of Jesus Christ. The spatial dimension of existence, therefore, can be understood in the light of a temporal model that is thoroughly eschatological, transforming the present because it is oriented toward the consummation when Christ will come again.

Why do we constantly speak of this mission as permission? It is a gift rather than a demand because the permission means that never again will we live in isolation, even though sometimes we may live with the illusion of loneliness. But Jesus promises, "Go therefore and make disciples of all nations . . . and lo, I am with you always, to the close of the age" (Matt. 28:19–20). It is a gift because it enables us to live within a new structure of existence, the transformed time in which the Spirit is present and active and the redeemed space which is no longer neutral or inimical but irrefutably our own because the permission has been spoken to us there. So people live alongside one another, some in the new time and some in the old, some with a place of their own and some with none, and outwardly they are no different. But even where there is massive uprootedness or the prospect of enduring joblessness or even the apparent disintegration of a whole tradition, Christians still have their location and their vocation. Neither the elaborate stratagems nor brute indifference of society can ever deprive them of these, or of the sovereign presence of him who promises that they shall never be left alone again but shall live with him forever.

Second, this freedom granted us by the Holy Spirit is inseparable from order, just as gospel is incomprehensible apart from law. The work of the Holy Spirit is not only to usher us into the new liberty of the children of God, but also to redeem the featureless and burdensome freedom that is the correlate of the loneliness of sin. Little is more desolating than the aimlessness that characterizes much of contemporary life: the withering of tradition to mere routine, the decline of tolerance to indifference, the confusion of freedom with refusal of commitment, and the confusion of the presence of limits with deprivation. In this context, we learn anew that mission is permission, because it invests our freedom with two requisites: the concretion and also the structure without which liberty means no more than isolation from everything that renders life worthwhile. The Christian mission is a gift because not only does placement by the gospel endow freedom with a necessary concreteness, but the authority of the law also invests these meetings with the moral structure that prevents them from becoming our surrender of ourselves to the needs of others or occasions for the demand that they surrender themselves to us.

The New Testament teaches that the gospel rescues us from the tyranny of the law, for now we need not fruitlessly seek to do for ourselves what Jesus Christ has already done. But it is equally true that the law is itself part and parcel of the gospel. The work of the Holy Spirit must be understood as a liberation that law and gospel achieve together, for without the former there is only the worst sort of captivity, the bondage to meaninglessness which is identical with disoriented liberty that has lost its center and structure. Apart from the work of reconciliation, the greatest instances of creative freedom we encounter are in the arts. No one knows better than the artist that whatever diminishes constraint diminishes strength, for such constraints as pigments, brushes, the notes of the scale, and the obduracy of words are the only instruments that freedom owns. In theological perspective, law is not an externally imposed limit upon us, but the single gate through which freedom can escape its helplessness, realize its potential, and find itself set free. This is a difficult lesson to

accept in the countries where there seems no relation between morality and the alleged rule of law, but there is a
difference between our contingent orders and the law of
God that we must honor and obey because it is the presupposition of reconciliation by the eternal Son.

Third, the freedom that the Spirit confers and the existence of Christian community are inseparable. Whatever is
said of the individual is necessarily subordinate to what
is said of the church, for the latter is no less crucial for the
formation of Christians than is natural community for the
growth of every self. We have seen that the achievement of
a sense of identity is always a gift from others. There is no
sense of the self that does not presuppose the presence of
others, no taste for the self that has not been inspired by
their caring, no development of agency apart from suffering the agency of others, no independence that has not
been nurtured by dependence, and no achievement of initiative except through responsiveness.

"The wages of sin is death" (Rom. 6:23), which is present
in anticipation in the separation of the sinner from other
creatures. This separation is a penalty not only because it
engenders our lacerating sense of loneliness, but much
more so because it means the actual erosion of our humanity, a reduction of our opportunities and diminishment of
our freedom, since the true form of the human is always
dialogical and not solitary. Once again we encounter the
truth that mission is permission, for it increases our possibilities because it brings us into new relationships not only
with those to whom the mission is directed but also with all
the others who have been allowed to engage in it, and not
only with creatures like ourselves but also with the triune
God. Through the Spirit, the risen Christ is present with us
in the midst of our earthly cares, anxieties, and preoccupa-
tions, quieting the din around us by the sound of his voice,
and renewing our perspective upon everything that had
seemed to cheat us of any perspective at all or else leave us
with none except its own.

Quite inevitably, then, the virtues which Christians describe as gifts of the Holy Spirit presuppose the community that the Spirit himself creates, and wither when they leave its embrace. Faith is unintelligible except in the light of the relational character of existence, for it is oriented to what lies beyond ourselves. Hope depends upon our relationships with others, for they provide the reasons for our hope. Our capacity to love rests upon the ways that we have antecedently been loved, and our ability to care upon the caring we have received. The self must be awarded a sense of its own worth by others if it is to be enabled to love, for the self that cannot value itself has no reason to value its neighbor. Just as community is the presupposition of a natural sense of identity and of every secular form of faith, hope, and love, so is it also indispensable for the cultivation of their Christian versions.

This community exists because "by one Spirit are we all baptized into one body, whether we be Jews or Gentiles, whether we be bond or free; and have been all made to drink into one Spirit" (1 Cor. 12:13 KJV). The true church is not sustained by the natural affinities among people that support the inherent exclusiveness of all other communities; instead, it is always biased toward those who have been outsiders, just as Jesus himself was an outsider both in his life and in the manner of his death. Because it belongs to him it is a community of reconciliation, and the inclusiveness of this reconciliation means that it always seeks to embrace more than those whom it has already touched. When the permission to engage in the mission is heard, the world is transformed by our placement, opportunities are expanded by the gospel's inclusive design, initiative is oriented by its gift of order, and therefore our freedom gains concreteness, enrichment, and structure—three requisites that freedom cannot give itself but is given by its risen Lord. All this and more is contained within the idea of reconciliation, which means not only the restoration of former community but also its increase, not only the return of lost possibilities but also their enlargement, not only release from the past but also the greater liberty offered by acknowledgment of the order God transforms for us through Jesus from enemy to ally.

The work of the Spirit has been summarized in many ways, but perhaps regeneration or new birth is the most satisfactory description, for these words return us explicitly to the familial imagery that is at the core of the biblical narrative. New birth always involves a double movement: justification and sanctification, dying with Christ and rising with him, repentance as mortification of the old self and vivification of the new. It is a reflection of and participation in the twofold journey of the Son: his humiliation and substitution of himself for us, his exaltation and sharing of his life with us. Unlike his life, however, ours is not a progression from one to the other; our redemption is an eschatological affair, and even the most stalwart disciple needs to ask forgiveness for continuing in sin.

Regeneration means relinquishing the quest to do for ourselves what he has done for us and accepting what he has done as always and *wholly* sufficient. Never again, no matter how great the weight of the world's evidence to the contrary, can we for a moment doubt that each of us is prized, loved beyond imagining, and purchased from sin and death at a cost not all the riches of the universe could ever pay. The work of the Spirit is to make real for us this exchange that Christ has wrought, bringing the old self to Calvary where Jesus stands in its place, and enabling the new self to grow ever more faithfully into his likeness within his community, where we taste in anticipation the perfect freedom of the children of God. The task of the Spirit is not to lead us into new truth, but to engraft us into the truth and life revealed once for all in the ministry, cross, and resurrection of Jesus. The Spirit is creative because of his relation to the exalted Lord, not in some other sense that is more or less independent of him.

The Spirit is Lord of the church and not at all a product of its immanent resources, for the church has neither righteousness nor beauty nor even particular utility of its own.

It is wholly the Spirit, not the community, that is finally the source of our faith, the ground of our hope, and the inspiration of our love. But the Spirit operates to form Christian persons through the community, not apart from it. One is the agent, the other the instrument. If the relation between them cannot be reversed, neither can it be broken: in this sense, at least, it is beyond dispute that "He who has not the church for his mother has not God for his Father." Only through the community does the Spirit impress upon us the truth of the story to which the community's life is owed, and only in the midst of the faithful are we enabled to continue in faith toward him whose everlasting fidelity overwhelms all our faithlessness so that it counts for nothing beside the majesty of his infinite and enduring grace.

Christian community is entirely different from voluntary associations of people who share particular aims and values. But it is like other groups in that it, too, involves relationships that are sustained only by a story or complex of stories which bind persons to one another so that they grow to share the same history. Just as community is the foundation of personality formation, so are stories the presuppositions and sustainers of significant community, whether human or divine. The biblical narrative of Jesus and the covenant that he completes is a story like many others, and yet so different in the mode of its relation to us that Christians must recognize the radical discontinuity between the dynamics of this community and all others. This statement is an expression of humility, not pride, for it is simply a confession that the story which binds us together *becomes* God's story for us, as well as our own story, only through an event occasioned by God himself. When the Spirit enables us to recognize it as the Word of God and submit ourselves to it, this insubstantial narrative reunifies and increases the community, which then itself becomes more faithfully the Spirit's instrument and more transparently the medium through which each of us and all of us together are united with the risen Lord.

Reflection upon the Holy Spirit must integrate a variety of themes that suffer distortion when they are approached independently of one another. His works must be understood in a unitive way, for he is the one who comes to unite. We must recognize the indissoluble relation of self and world, gospel and law, individual and community, as well as the inseparability of them all. Their integration is evident in our permission for a mission, for this gift of the Spirit bestows upon the freedom that the Spirit himself brings a concreteness, structure, and richness that we can never find for ourselves. Christian liberty must in no way be equated with the loosening of constraints, for then it finally grows indistinguishable from aimlessness and arbitrariness, which are only new forms of bondage to ourselves.

In the end, however, it is not reflection but *prayer* that is the key to everything. In prayer alone, as the Spirit himself speaks for us and listens within us, as we ourselves are drawn into the richness of God's own life, we come to learn more than the dull blade of our language can ever convey. It is in silence and adoration that the Spirit ultimately discloses himself and teaches us again the familiar axiom that although God can always be addressed, the splendor of his nature can never be adequately expressed, for no tongue can convey the incandescent love for one another of Father, Son, and Spirit, perfectly One and blessed Trinity.

8

"The Holy Catholic Church . . . and the Life Everlasting"

His Story as Ours

Just as God's decision for us is bound up forever with the flesh and blood of a particular man, Jesus of Nazareth, so is the Spirit who brings us to the Son irrevocably related not only to a particular historical community but also to certain finite and definite media through which Jesus discloses himself to his people. These media, in addition to the Bible, are preaching, the sacraments, liturgy, and prayer, each of which is meant first of all to be a faithful expression of the story of Jesus Christ. All of them derive their legitimacy and character from the biblical narrative through which the Spirit binds together the church. But the identification of the Spirit with these particular forms does not mean that now he is made captive of the community that is his own creation. He remains its sovereign Lord.

We have insisted that the Christian story differs from all others because the apprehension of it as the Word of God rather than merely as an artful narrative depends upon God alone. The media that are subordinate to the Scriptures function in the same way: they become revelation for us in an event that is contingent upon divine initiative and not the result of powers delegated to the community itself. It was in order to emphasize this priority of divine action that Martin Luther distinguished between the hiddenness of God and God in his revelation. The distinction was not elaborated in order to contrast a time when people did not know God with a new time in which they do, but to stress that God is hidden in Jesus Christ and in the Bible in such fashion that he cannot be recognized by reason alone. God comes among us in his revelation in a way that contradicts all our expectations, and so we cannot acknowledge his presence without his aid.

But emphasis upon God's sovereignty pays him no honor if it obscures the magnitude of his grace in choosing certain elements of our world to serve each day as media of the Spirit until the time of consummation. So it is proper to speak of the literal inspiration of Scripture, for example, for just as God's redemptive work cannot ever be separated from the blood and bone of an individual man, neither can his Word to us be severed from the human words of the book that bears witness to Jesus Christ. But we can speak in this way of the inspiration of Scripture only when it is understood as our master and not our possession, as the book of the whole historical community and not of our generation alone. Whenever claims about the authority of the Bible are divorced from reflection upon the Spirit, a dead book supplants a living Lord and salvation really becomes a human achievement instead of the work of grace.

The other media of the Spirit are also meant to reflect something of the form as well as the substance of the biblical narrative, and this double fidelity is crucial because community is jeopardized when its stories grow thin or dissolve into mere statements of beliefs. Each of these media involves the Christian in at least a fourfold relation: to God's work at Calvary and Easter morning, to other members of the community, to God's action in the contemporary world, and to those who do not yet know that Christ has died for them. Each is a medium of grace in many ways, but not least of all because of its function as an interpretive device, setting forth the person and work of Christ so that his presence can be recognized in the midst of the world today.

This fourfold reference is apparent in the Lord's Supper, for example. It proclaims the forgiveness of sins and the imminence of the consummation, directing our attention toward both the past and the future of our risen Lord. The bread and wine are also tokens that in this world all things come from our Father in heaven, that the whole earth is at his disposal, and that he has adopted us as his children. Moreover, the Eucharist provides motive and occasion for Christian parents and children to forgive one another for their simple humanness, as well as for their betrayal of the human. This cup is offered for the forgiveness of the betrayal of the child by the human parent, of the parent by the child, and of the divine Father by them both. This bread is offered for the humanizing of all expectations of what is human, so that we will no longer ask too much of it, as well as for the strengthening of faith in the divine. The meal of reconciliation, then, is offered for the reconciling of family meals far beyond the sanctuary. Furthermore, the Christ who comes to his people in this event is the new Adam who bears all people in himself; so the meal is also celebrated for the redemption of the potential exclusiveness of familial imagery and always orients the community toward a family greater still.

The act at the center of the devotional life of the church challenges it with the permission of its mission, thrusts it into the midst of the world where so many have not heard the good news of the gospel, and furnishes indispensable interpretive resources for discerning the presence and deciphering the will of the Lord. The means of grace through which the Spirit nourishes the church provide the tools without which engagement with the world means nothing more than the blind leading the blind, all vulnerable to whatever voice cries, "Lo, here is Christ; or, lo, he is there . . . to seduce, if it were possible, even the elect" (Mark 13:21–22 KJV). The Christian theologian, however, can speak with authority only of the operations of the Spirit within the Christian community. In acknowledging the wider sphere where God's work is so frequently hidden from us, perhaps the one certainty is that he who has dealt with us in an incomparably merciful and loving fashion, despite all our ingratitude, unloveliness, and incessant betrayals, can surely chip through the hardness of every human heart. When we cannot discern his presence outside our community, perhaps the reason is that we have sought to make the means of grace captives of the church instead of instruments for the broadening of the church's vision. Even in the midst of the world, certainly, the wideness of his mercy is "like the wideness of the sea."

"The Holy catholic Church." The Christian community has traditionally distinguished itself from others by speaking of the four marks of the church. Only two are cited in the Creed, but the others are implied. The church is *holy* because it is the creation of the Holy Spirit. It is intrinsically no more righteous than the sinners who comprise it, but holiness is conferred upon it as a gift that foreshadows the consummation of all things when the fullness of the Spirit will be poured out upon the creation. The church is *catholic* in the sense that it is universal, extending through many generations and many lands. More important, it is catholic because no one is barred by class, caste, race, or past. As the body of Christ the reconciler, it exists to unite all people, all communities, all races and nations, rich and poor, deprived and privileged, broken and strong.

Because it is holy and catholic, the church is also *one;* it is the sphere of the Holy Spirit, and the Spirit frees only as he unites. Unity does not mean uniformity, however; it is an eschatological affair, present now as a foretaste of what is still to come, when we shall be united with all the company of heaven. Finally, the church is *apostolic:* it proclaims the gospel entrusted to the apostles, it pursues the mission awarded to the original apostolic community, and the functions of its ministers are no different than those of the apostles themselves. But this is not guaranteed by a historical succession of pastors or bishops; it is realized when the proclamation of the apostolic gospel and prosecution of its mission constitute the community as one, holy, and catholic. The other marks of the church are entirely dependent upon the apostolic preaching that the Spirit alone renders possible because it is God's Word and not man's.

The contents of the third article can initially appear unrelated, as though they had been chosen from among many equally important possibilities. So we must explore the logic of their selection and their intrinsic connections. Necessarily, the first reference is to the church, for entrance to community reverses the loneliness of sin and is the presupposition of freedom. The description of the community as holy and catholic emphasizes both its distinction from the world and the inclusiveness of the work of reconciliation that is the warrant for its mission. The Creed places the Holy Spirit and the community beside one another, for the New Testament insists upon the absolute inseparability of communion with the Spirit and community with other creatures—but only in that order, for the Spirit is always first.

"The Communion of Saints; The Forgiveness of sins." The first of these phrases is in apposition to the portrayal of the church as holy and the second to its description as catholic. The original significance of *communio sanctorum* is obscure, for the Latin can refer either to the community or to its worship. What is more important, however, is that either interpretation affirms that the church is set apart from the world. Were it not, it could bring nothing to the world except what the world already possesses. Community is not inherently liberating in our fallen realm. Every human group can stifle and suffocate its members, teaching them to see themselves as nothing but the sum of their roles and functions within it, perpetuating the terrible illusion that the freedom of some people can be built upon the suffering of others. Christians are able to speak of community as the *prius* of freedom *only* because their community is not their own creation but the product of the work of the Holy Spirit, and it is ordered not by the will to power and quest for security but by the truth, light, and righteousness of the everlasting Lord.

As *communio sanctorum*, then, the church is set apart. This separation is never an end in itself, however, but always a means to a greater end, the fulfillment of the mission entrusted to it by Jesus Christ. As the company of the elect, the church is elected for service: those who are touched by the unitive Spirit, and addressed by the Lord who bears all people in himself and promises to draw all unto himself, are set apart by the permission to give themselves to a mission. So these ambiguous words that in one way or another stress the separation of the community constrain the church to reflect upon the reasons for it, and to recognize anew that the opportunity to serve is part of the promise of freedom, for through it we are placed in a fashion that means the redemption of one of the structures of finite life, our space together.

The forgiveness of sins is the core of the biblical narrative that is sketched for us in the second article, the substance of the missionary proclamation of the church, and the presupposition of the concluding words of the third article, for there can be no future at all for us unless we are able to speak of forgiveness. If there is no forgiveness, we remain locked in the past, prisoners of previous mistakes and misunderstandings, unable ever to begin again. Apart from forgiveness, all hope of creativity is gone; the risks involved in creativeness are beyond imagining without the assurance that it is possible to find reconciliation on the far side of our failures, betrayals, and all the hurts that we inflict. Without forgiveness there can be no enduring community of any sort. Without it, everything remains as fractured as ever, and the conflicts must still rage among those who, like ourselves, are enemies and strangers, sinners and ungodly. But forgiveness cannot be embraced without a deepened awareness of the importance of order and of the guilt incurred by its violation. So these words remind us of the structure without which creaturely freedom is no more than illusion, of the inseparability of law and gospel, and of the importance of constraints if indeterminate freedom is to be set truly free.

"The Resurrection of the body." Here is the promise that the glorious ending of the biblical story of Jesus is also intended for you and for all of us together. As we have died with him, so shall we one day be raised to live with him in his kingdom at the right hand of the Father. The promise of resurrection reinforces what is implicit in the mention of forgiveness and parallels the reference to *communio sanctorum,* in the sense that it affirms the present as well as future redemption of time in the same way that the latter implies the redemption of space by the gift of our mission.

Time is redeemed now, even though only in part and as a promise of what lies ahead, by the incandescence of a sense of an ending that releases us from the burden of apparent endlessness, invests with narrative structure what hitherto seemed irremediably episodic, and provides motivation to struggle in the present against whatever conflicts with the promised consummation. The Spirit who bears witness to Jesus Christ is himself the movement into the present of a future consummation of the whole creation, when Jesus will come again and we will be transformed into the likeness of the eternal Son.

No longer need we lie to ourselves that what we now enjoy will endure forever. It will not—but it will be returned to us. No longer need we spend our time inventing new ways to disguise the reality of death. We will die, you and I and all those for whom we have given the most precious days of our lives—but we shall live again, in God. No longer need we curse the serial character of time, draining away from us the fragile joys of existence until they are lost even from the terrain of memory. They vanish like sparks in the night despite all our stratagems—but the strands of our time will be knit together again. No longer need we hasten by mirrors that reflect the evanescence of our suppleness, strength, youth, and beauty. There is no help for limbs twisted and withered by age— but we shall be made new. No longer need we ignore the epiphany of our destiny as sinners in each farewell, every misunderstanding, every averted glance, all interruptions that leave us ever more alone. We will be solitary in the earth—but then there will be all the company of heaven. Death will come, and many of its guises are terrible, indeed. Beyond its advent, however, there will be another, the second advent of him who is Lord of death as well as Lord of life, and into whose hands we commend our spirits, now and forever.

In summary. The Holy Spirit frees us by means of a community that is set apart from the world in order to worship God and serve the world, and its mission places us in such fashion that our featureless or too crowded space is trans-

formed. The Spirit unites the church with the Lord who
will come again, and by whom we are provided with a sense
of an ending that redeems the time between the times of
beginning and end. Because it belongs to Jesus Christ, this
is a community of reconciliation, and from the miracle of
our reconciliation we learn our enduring dependence
upon the law of God, which is itself so much a creative
determinant of freedom that it must be seen as a part of
the gospel. The reference to the community as holy and
catholic is expanded in many ways by the two phrases that
follow it. Even though it is the promise of resurrection that
complements *communio sanctorum* by speaking of the redemption of the second of the structures of our existence,
it must be preceded by the mention of forgiveness. The
latter begins the renewal of time because without it there is
no way into the future at all. These four phrases, then—
beginning with the church and concluding with the resurrection—focus upon community and freedom, which are
the great twin works of the Spirit, in their inseparability
from forgiveness and law, and implicitly upon the redemption of space and time through the missionary proclamation of the story of Jesus. Such is the unity and logic, at
least in part, of the article.

Before turning to the conclusion of the Creed, there are
three topics that require brief attention. First, in the initial
words of the article the church explicitly acknowledges the
triune nature of its Lord. Now, as the Creed speaks of the
incorporation of the creature into what God has done,
each successive phrase reflects the reality of three distinct
and yet inseparable divine modes of being. This community is constituted by the Spirit who eternally bears witness to
the risen Son in whom the Father has been disclosed.
Through the Spirit we are made recipients of the forgiveness offered because the Father came in the Son to reconcile the world to himself. The final expressions of the
Christian hope turn our attention to the Father who is the
source of all life, to the Son who reveals him and through
whom we are born again into new life, and so to the Spirit
whose presence guarantees the fulfillment of our existence

beyond the grave. Every element of the article, at least in an indirect fashion, reaffirms the trinitarian character of the God in whom Christians believe.

Second, redemption is a temporal affair, not release from temporality. Just as the second article concludes with three affirmations in different tenses, so does the third bring together past, present, and future, and then deliver them together to eternity. Community refers to the present, forgiveness to the past, resurrection to the future. But community and forgiveness also await us in eternity, while we have already died and have been raised again in and with Jesus Christ. The tenses interpenetrate in such a way that we see within the article itself a reflection of God's victory over the atomized and fragmented character of time under the curse. The past is retrieved from its pastness and becomes a contemporary reality through the Spirit, while the same Spirit imports the future into the present as a fundamental determinant of what we now can do. The past is no longer what is lost to us or else still imprisons us; the future is no longer unknown, or powerless because it is merely future. Instead, the present is filled by the power of what is yet to come and renewed by the reality of the forgiveness that now is never past, because the Son eternally intercedes for us at the Father's right hand.

This portrayal of the redemption of time through the Spirit invites us to live in the present as if the end had come and as if the present were not. "As if . . . as if not" is the essential form that life must assume in the light of the eschatological gospel. No matter whether the permission is interpreted in a conservative or revolutionary way, persons who are invited to live as if the new were come and the old had passed away must understand themselves in a radically different fashion. They can no longer define themselves in the world's terms, "for ye are dead, and your life is hid with Christ in God" (Col. 3:3 KJV). But this new life is future, too, and so we must continue to see ourselves as still sinners, even though we are forgiven. It is impossible to hear the "as if . . . as if not" without a renewed awareness that the self is not as it would like itself to be; the invitation, therefore, directs our attention again to the question of our fidelity to the Christian imagery of the self that we have been enabled through the Spirit to espouse. So we are challenged at the conclusion of the Creed to examine our actual correspondence with the avowal of identity with which the Creed begins.

Third, perhaps it is necessary to ask whether this treatment of the third article suggests that in fact it is finally reducible to a catalog of beliefs. The answer must be firmly negative; the whole of it simply asserts our own incorporation through the Spirit into the narrative sketched in the second article, so that our ambiguous careers gain their coherence and real meaning from outside themselves. The reference to forgiveness, especially, is not one item among many for us to believe but a reminiscence and summary of the whole story that has now become not only the story of Jesus but also and entirely our own. This representation of the interpenetration of time future and time past invites us to offer our own contributions in the present to the completion of God's design by living from and toward the sense of an ending the narrative provides—and so to express in our intentions and actions, and thereby confirm, this new identity that we have declared in a public place and public way.

"And the Life everlasting." In turning to these concluding words we must ask not only what they mean but also why they should have been included at all. Is it not sufficient to end with the affirmation of the resurrection of the dead? During the early centuries of Christianity, it was frequently believed that existence did not terminate with death. What was really in dispute was the nature or quality of life after death: was it a shadowy, tenuous mode of existence and thus reason for despair, or was it something more? In this context, the expression of Christian hope in the language of the resurrection of the body held a double significance. On the one hand, it affirmed that bodily existence is appropriate for the creature; this world is not a prison of the spirit but a proper home for the people whom God has

made. On the other, the focus upon resurrection implied with equal force that ultimately we have no home within this world but can find fulfillment only somewhere else. The addition of "life everlasting" dissipates any ambiguity about our condition after death has had its way with us, for it proclaims a qualitative transformation of existence and, most important, it directs our attention away from ourselves and again toward him in whom life has its source and completion.

The emphasis of the last words lies upon *life,* not its qualifier; the adjective does not denote endlessness, for that is the condition from which creaturely time must be redeemed, but the radical difference and perfect quality of the gift of new life that will be oriented wholly toward God. Christians have always confessed that we now know a relationship to the Eternal so intimate and profound that we are persuaded not even death can destroy it. So there is a clear Christian answer to the perennial human question, "whether the things we care for most are at the mercy of the things we care for least." But this is not the question with which the Creed is concerned, for its words direct us not toward the ambiguous intimations of our own experience but toward the sovereign reality of God and his triumphant work in Jesus Christ. He who is Lord of death as well as Lord of life is the Coming One, not only a presence above, beneath, or behind us but one who always beckons us forward to new communion with himself. After the consummation it shall be everlasting, no longer liable to the interruptions that mark failed time, time under the curse.

Nevertheless, although the adjective emphasizes the discontinuity between life as we know it now and the future of the children of God, it is important to recognize at least three elements of continuity. First, life everlasting means the fulfillment of the new mode of existence and altered sense of identity that are present possessions of those who have died with Christ in baptism and have been born anew through the Spirit. It describes the completion of a relationship that is already more real to the eyes of faith than everything we can encounter in the everyday world. Because life everlasting is the unveiling of our present but hidden incorporation into the crucified and risen Jesus Christ, it is a continuation of our lives as Christians and not a venture into an unknown and wholly alien realm.

Second, we have constantly stressed that the communication of the Spirit is inseparably related to the creation of community. The final words of the Creed not only designate a corporate fulfillment but also clearly imply, because this is the fruition of life in Christ, that there can be no fulfillment at all apart from other people. The dialogical form of creaturely life denotes our eternal destiny even more than it describes the proper shape of existence in this world. As the antithesis and overthrow of death, life everlasting means life together. So this conclusion must never be regarded as though it could be a selfish hope, but only as a confession that there is, indeed, no hope at all unless it is for you and me together and not the self alone.

Finally, not only in order to understand life everlasting but also to grasp the dimensions of Christian responsibility in the contemporary world, we must underscore a third continuity. When humanity discovers anew its lost center as it is incorporated into the history of the one individual who is also a universal, God's only Son, the world that does not possess its center in itself begins, through our redemption, to find its proper unity. Because life everlasting means that "we shall be also in the likeness of his resurrection" (Rom. 6:5 KJV), it affirms the renewal not only of the creature but, through the creature, of the whole creation over which Jesus reigns. The beginning of the transformation of the structure of finite life through the provisions of a mission and of a sense of an ending offers its own testimony that there can be no salvation for us apart from the restoration of our world. So these last words have a cosmic reference, insisting upon the involvement of what is other than human in the process of human redemption. They warn us not to despoil the world but to cherish it as also the object of God's love and focus of his concern.

Is it not unimaginable that God should redeem the creatures he has chosen as his deputies and care no longer for all he has placed in their hands? How could we ever find fulfillment without a world? We must always be its faithful stewards and caretakers. The realm of the finite and definite, with all the constraints that invest our liberty with meaning and elicit our greatest inventiveness, and despite the savagery with which it sometimes assaults its most defenseless citizens, still has God as its author; it shall not be left behind. The reality of the new creation constrains us to care not only for the creature but also for the whole universe, which "was subjected to futility, not of its own will but by the will of him who subjected it in hope; because the creation itself will be set free from its bondage to decay and obtain the glorious liberty of the children of God" (Rom. 8:20–21).

The new life that is even now a partial possession points toward the time when Christ shall come again in glory; then the remnants of loneliness and separation will finally yield to the communion and community of everlasting life. The last words proclaim again the omnipotence and creativity disclosed in God's work of reconciliation, where he has revealed his power perfectly to fulfill all his fatherly purposes and the fatherliness of all his purposes. Life everlasting means that sin is ended and overthrown. So the gospel of the forgiveness of sins looks forward to the day when the Father will decree that sin shall be no more, when the frailty of our faith will be embraced in the faithfulness of his strength, and when we shall be enabled to say—not in anticipation but in retrospect, not in the accents of a particular church but with all the company of heaven, not as an article of faith but as the sum and substance of our whole vision—"that neither death, nor life, nor angels, nor principalities, nor powers, nor things present, nor things to come, nor height, nor depth, nor any other creature, shall be able to separate us from the love of God, which is in Christ Jesus our Lord" (Rom. 8:38–39 KJV). To him, whose presence is the greatest of his presents, with the Father and the Holy Spirit, Blessed Trinity, be all glory, praise, and honor, now and forever.

9

Epilogue: Christian People

Imagery of Selfhood

Perhaps it is appropriate to comment briefly upon the resources the Creed offers for the development of a Christian sense of character by those who employ it as an identity avowal. The question of resources, as we argued in the first chapter, is really a matter of images of the self. They are the elements of a sense of identity and, because conduct expresses and confirms a certain sense of selfhood, they provide the reasons why we choose to exercise our freedom as we do. We originally claimed that the master image of the child of God possesses little content and is inherently ambiguous; for its legitimation, clarification, and amplification it depends upon the sketch of the biblical narrative in the second article. In the light of this story, for example, it is evident that it must not be understood in a way that implies immaturity and the absence of accountability.

Because we have not continued to pursue the question of a Christian sense of identity in a systematic fashion, however, we have had little opportunity to show in detail how the narrative not only justifies and controls the image of the child of God, but also amplifies it by a gift of additional master images that crystallize more of the significance of the story for self-understanding. Although the story is regulative in relation to portrayals of the self, it will fail to shape our conduct decisively unless it finds expression in one sort of master imagery or another. The form of the Christian life can neither be derived directly from the uninterpreted narrative and the image of the child, nor explored faithfully in abstraction from them. The task, then, is to find in and through the story master images that can define our freedom to live in Christ today and enrich our initial representation of the Christian self. Because it attempts to address a question with which the Creed is not directly concerned, this epilogue should be omitted by those whose interests are confined to the text itself. In part, it is no more than a summary of what has already been said, but now this material must be organized for different ends.

What we need is not a single image but two complementary representations of the self, one of which expresses the implications for identity and agency of the first advent of the Son of God while the other conveys those of the advent that is still to come. In the end, these two focuses are everything: what he has been and done for us, and what he shall do when he comes again. "Jesus Christ is the same yesterday and today and for ever" (Heb. 13:8), but there is a difference between his humiliation and his exaltation. This distinction has its consequences for understanding the Christian life: the self must be seen as the recipient of grace in relation to God's reconciling work, and also as responsive to grace in the light of the approaching consummation of all things. If we need no less than two new master images, however, neither do we need more. We do not mean to suggest that even in dealing with master images one can choose as many as one prefers, in the light of one's own sometimes idiosyncratic inclinations, from an almost inexhaustible procession.

These twin portrayals of the Christian person, together with that of the child, will exhibit a certain resemblance to the heuristic device that offers us an initial perspective within the biblical narrative—the doctrine of the *Triplex Munus,* or threefold role of Jesus as prophet, priest, and king. A certain resemblance is inevitable if, in fact, Jesus is the new Adam in whom the meaning of humanness is perfectly disclosed and into whom we are incorporated through the Holy Spirit. On the other hand, the correlation will be no more than approximate, for a heuristic device is simply a point of orientation. Furthermore, those who are in Christ are certainly not summoned to enact his career anew, as though we were constrained to do for ourselves what he has already done. The identity and vocation of those who are in Christ are not the same as his, for we need add nothing to what he has accomplished.

As a preface to exploration of the other master images that the narrative provides, it is important to remind ourselves of an argument in the third chapter on the first article, to the effect that the figure of the child requires qualification by the image of the Christian as inheritor or deputy—even though the most profound justification for this does not emerge until the concluding references of the Creed to resurrection and life everlasting. The eschatological promise of the gospel is offered not only to us but, for our sake, also to the world, which we are therefore called to cultivate and cherish as a context delegated to us by the Father of all. A deputy is a person whose authority depends upon fidelity to someone else, whose domain is not a possession but a trust, and whose exercise of power is not a right but a privilege. In its loose correlation with the prophetic office of Christ, the image tells of one who speaks and acts authoritatively, but whose authority derives from hearing and speaking a word that is always other than his own and that he too must obey.

This portrait of the self divests the master image of its potential suggestion of privilege without responsibility, includes an appeal for resourcefulness and for creativity, and incorporates into the gospel of our adoption a command and obedience model of humanity that is mandated by the recognition of the sovereignty of God. Nevertheless, this is a subordinate image and, while it seriously qualifies the meaning of the figure of the child, it does not share the same status. The image implied by the root metaphor expresses what has now become irrevocable, though by grace alone, for the adopted child is destined to remain forever the child of this Father. The secondary image of inheritor or deputy tells us of the radical contingency of the dominion of the children of God within the world. The

primary portrayal of the self provides the irrevocable justification for the secondary, while the secondary expresses
something that is wholly contingent and therefore the
image itself shares this same contingency.

The first of the complementary master images that must
be found emerges from the Creed with its own overwhelm-
ing necessity: it is the representation of the self as
sufferer. Because we have devoted much attention to suffering, however, now we need do no more than briefly
summarize what has already been said. No other description of the march of Jesus toward Calvary is really compar-
able, for the meaning of the exchange through which our
redemption is achieved is that he suffers in our place and
for our sake because he constantly suffers the Father's initiative and is perfectly responsive to it. Because he is a new
Adam, the true form of our humanity is also disclosed as
suffering: it means being for and being with, in obedience
to the Father.

We have seen that the gospel affirms continuities as well
as stressing the discontinuity between Christian existence
and the life of the sinner. So it is inevitable that this new
master image should also reflect fundamental realities of
the human situation everywhere and always. We suffer
when we come into the world and we suffer when we leave
it, and between our entrance and our exit it is only through
suffering that we find whatever fulfillment the world has
apportioned for us. There is no way to describe the original situation of the newborn except as an instance of suffering, for the child is wholly dependent upon the initiatives
of others for its survival, for the first expressions of its own
agency, and for the development of the initial intimations
of its identity. We have insisted that suffering provides a
neutral image that suggests both gain and loss, however,
and which awaits definition by the character of the initiatives and obstacles that the self encounters. On the one
hand, therefore, it is entirely justified by our ordinary experience and is a perfect correlate of the representation of
the self as child; on the other, as a theological image its

neutrality means that it is amenable to definition strictly by reference to the career of Jesus Christ.

Even when the initiatives we encounter seem bent upon our repression or exploitation, suffering is not without its creative possibilities; constraints can foster strength, and obstacles engender patience and creativity. It is the determination of our freedom that frees us, and this is the consequence of the presence of others. Placement is a gift, even in the worst of times when all the voices that arrest us ask that we serve their purposes rather than our own, insofar as it liberates us from our egocentricity, awakens us to the diversity of human community, and confronts us with the possibility of judgment from perspectives different than our own. We come to possess more of ourselves through the offering of ourselves that the presence of others requires, and often even when their interests seem inimical to our own—simply because the offering strengthens and affirms the inescapably relational form of personal life. At every juncture, we learn that limitation constitutes not only our fate but also new opportunities for enrichment and the greater realization of freedom—and so it must be if the self is made for God, if it is incorporated into the way of Jesus Christ, and if the true form of the personal is dialogical and communal, not solitary.

The final master image must explicitly convey what the figures of the child and the sufferer cannot directly express, which is the eschatological cast of every aspect of the Christian vision. We await the second advent of the risen Lord and it is the sense of an ending provided by the promise of his return that enables us to decipher parts of the divine design amidst the jumble of the time between the times. This promise is at the center of the portrayal of Christian life in the New Testament, as we have seen, and especially in the Pauline letters, as the permission to live "as if . . . as if not." The need for an image of the self that can express this fundamental orientation of life in Christ is scarcely open to dispute. The argument of a book that preceded this essay, *Images for Self-Recognition,* was that the representation of the self as player is the most satisfactory of many and various possibilities. There is no other image that can so richly capture the invitation to live against appearances and as though the earth were other than it is, to see others and ourselves from a perspective that nothing in the world can entirely legitimate, to act as though we were what we are not yet and as other than we are, and to transform the present by living in relation to a future age when the power and glory of God will be everywhere disclosed and every tongue will praise his name.

The figure of the player displays many affinities with the ancient representation of the Christian as a pilgrim, but it anchors the Christian life much more firmly in the density of everyday experience. It is also more integrally related to the imagery of the self as sufferer and child, for play is especially the prerogative of childhood and is, indeed, the first expression of the child's responsiveness to suffering the initiatives of others. Playing is an instinct written into every animal and, along with the household or family, a universal instrument of socialization. Perhaps no other image could suggest more strongly our need for order and boundaries, and the importance of rules if the self is to find freedom and express its own inventiveness. Structure is indispensable to play: no matter whether the choice of it belongs to the player himself or is originally exercised by someone else, the binding of the self by itself to some order that is consonant with fairness is inseparable from fulfillment and freedom. So, although it is associated first of all with childhood it is far from childish, for it tutors us in the importance of justice as fairness or fair play.

On the other hand, our appetite for play can express itself in many disorderly ways that set persons against one another and ravage our common life. Some similitudes of play seem dedicated to the destruction of every order, simply for the pleasure of it. This image, like that of the sufferer, is initially neutral or ambiguous, and so it is amenable to definition strictly in the light of the promised consummation and the present activity of the Holy Spirit.

Theologically considered, the figure of the player counsels that we must be less than wholly serious about the self and its world as appearances disclose them, for God's revelation means that he alone can now be regarded with the unqualified seriousness that we once lavished upon our own projects and purposes. Neither can we continue to regard ourselves or others as nothing more than a sum of functions and roles, for we are addressed by our Father without reference to caste, clan, status, or role.

In its loose correlation with the kingly office of Christ, the image affirms that we are no longer ruled by the appearances of this world. But it not only expresses the freedom from the world offered by the opportunity to live from and toward a consummation beyond the world; it also affirms our responsibility in the present to exhibit in all our functions and roles nothing less than fidelity to the dictates of justice as fair play. Because everyone is at least potentially a player as the sphere of reconciliation constantly expands, the image will not condone less than fairness to all.

Far more important than anything else, however, is its capacity to express in a concrete and vivid way the permission that we are granted through the Spirit to transform our world by rendering the promise of the consummation a power in the present and, in the light of the imminent end, offering our own creaturely contributions to the completion of God's redemptive design. Such play is not a flight from the present but engagement with the possibilities that the present itself enshrines in relation to the second advent of him who promises to make all things new. But it is only a child whose innocence has not been enlightened by experience who can play for long in a world where shadows so frequently obscure the sun, where all playing is vulnerable to a thousand interruptions, and where some malign presence so often waits to assault those who are intent only upon their private games. The figure of the player can finally be legitimated in a world of randomness and accidents only by the presence of God, sustained only by communion with him who assures a consummation that permits us to live "as if . . . as if not," and changed only by grace from a reflection of the will of the individual into submission to the Father's purpose.

The complementary character of the twin images of player and sufferer, which perhaps begins with their shared testimony to the involution of freedom and limitation, has many facets. The figure of the sufferer can represent the self's capacity for love, while the figure of the player can express the self's commitment to justice. The first can display the self in its responsiveness to other selves and to God; the second can portray the self in its affirmation of the structures or laws without which all relationships are spoiled. The figure of the sufferer can depict the self in relation to the sovereign presence of God, while that of the player can convey the relationship of the self to its world in consequence of God's disclosure of himself. The one can emphasize the responsible self, the other the self as creative. The first stresses the relational or dialogical character of life, the second the inseparability of dialogical life from order.

The image of the sufferer captures the form of the journey of the Son of God from Bethlehem to Calvary, and the other expresses the sort of existence that is permitted for those who anticipate his coming again as judge and king. The former has its focus upon reconciliation, the latter upon resurrection and consummation; together, they can set forth in a unified fashion the implications of the first and second advents of Jesus Christ for the formation of a Christian sense of identity and character. The correlation of suffering with the priestly role of Jesus requires no commentary. The correlation of play with his kingly office concerns not only our liberation from the realm of appearances but also our opportunities for creativeness. Because he reigns, we are no longer ruled by the appearances of this world; because his reign is an eschatological reality that is still veiled, however, there is room and time for our own agency to offer its unsubstitutable contributions to the final shape of his kingdom.

The child of God, the sufferer, the player: perhaps they do not emerge with equally incontestable inevitability in the course of an explication of the Creed, but they seem nonetheless its richest implicates for the development of a Christian sense of personal identity. The disclosure of the Father in his only Son means that we become also his children by adoption. Suffering summarizes the exchange through which our reconciliation is achieved and provides the way by which we as well as the Son can come to the Father. Play is our acknowledgment of and creaturely contribution to the transformation of time present by the activity of the Spirit who is himself the content of the future consummation of the kingdom of God.

The earliest life of a child is pure suffering, for it is helpless apart from others, but from this suffering there develops a capacity for responsiveness that is expressed in its play. As the child of God discovers liberty and inventiveness through its play in response to the activity of the Spirit, it is enabled to live ever more faithfully in relation to the time when its hidden Lord will fulfill all things: it learns to exist "as if . . . as if not" as its suffering and play are ever more profoundly defined by the presence of the Spirit and the Son. Because they reflect the original and enduring situation of the individual within the family or household and complement the figure of the child of God, the portrayals of the self as sufferer and player contribute in their own ways to the strengthening of the familial character of the imagery of Christian faith which is demanded by its root metaphor of God as Father of the only Son and Father by adoption of us all.

There are many criteria, as we have suggested, by which the adequacy of these images must be assessed. Do they witness severally and together to the inseparability of freedom and community and order, of limitation and mission and fulfillment, of the relational and eschatological aspects of life? Is there real harmony or potential dissonance among them? Do they elicit and reconcile with one another a great variety of subordinate images? Do the figures of player and sufferer clothe the image of the child as richly as possible with the implications of the biblical narrative for the development of Christian character? Do they bind that controlling image ever more firmly to the density and detail of the story of the New Testament?

In the end, nothing matters except that the life of the imagination, like all other life, must serve the purposes of God. But the health and fidelity of the imagination are particularly important, because upon it so much else depends. Our conduct is shaped by the condition of our vision; we are free to choose or to struggle against only what we can see. Our vision, however, is determined by the most important images of the self from which we have fashioned our sense of identity. These furnish us with our perspectives upon everything else; they finally legislate not only what we will and what we will not see, but the particular angle or point of view from which the whole of reality will be assessed. How we see ourselves, then, determines how we will conduct ourselves in relation to others, to the world, and even to God—and all this is ultimately a matter of images. If we cannot see ourselves as Christians, we shall scarcely be able to act except in ways that the fashions of this world legitimate.

Others must decide whether or not the master images proposed in these pages can crystallize much of the significance of the biblical narrative for life in the world today. What is not a matter for dispute, however, is that if we cannot find sufficient resources for the formation of a Christian sense of identity that will sustain us not only in good times but also in days of confusion, pain, and loss, our lives will not offer all they might to the symphony of praise by the church universal to the limitless condescension and unfailing grace of him who has come and will come again in triumph and who, with the Father and the Holy Spirit, ever one God, lives and reigns now and forever.